MAN IN THE PAST, T]
AND THE FUT

The Evolution of Co:

THE SUN-INITIATION OF
THE DRUID PRIEST AND HIS
MOON-SCIENCE

ſ

MAN IN THE PAST, THE PRESENT AND THE FUTURE

The Evolution of Consciousness

Three lectures given in Stuttgart
14th, 15th, 16th September, 1923
Translated by E. Goddard

THE SUN-INITIATION OF THE DRUID PRIEST AND HIS MOON-SCIENCE

Lecture given in Dornach, 10th September, 1923

RUDOLF STEINER

RUDOLF STEINER PRESS
LONDON

First English Edition   1966
Second English Edition 1982

Translated from shorthand reports unrevised by the lecturer. The lectures are included in a volume of the Complete Centenary Edition of the works of Rudolf Steiner entitled: *Der Mensch in Vergangenheit, Gegenwart und Zukunft*. (Vol. No. 228 in the *Bibliographical Survey*, 1961).
This English edition is published in agreement with the Rudolf Steiner Nachlassverwaltung, Dornach, Switzerland.

Statistical Publishing House
Printed in Hungary

CONTENTS

FOREWORD

The following lectures were given by Rudolf Steiner shortly after his visit to Great Britain in August, 1923, and continue the theme of the evolution of consciousness which had been the subject of the lecture-course in Penmaenmawr, North Wales.* Particular reference to Druidic culture had been made during the course and the fourth lecture in the present volume has been included for that reason.

*   *   *   *

In connection with the publication of reports of lectures which were given as oral communications and not originally intended for print, Rudolf Steiner constantly emphasised the distinction between such reports on the one hand and his written works on the other. He reminded readers that certain premises were taken for granted when the words were spoken. "These premises," he wrote, "include at the very least the anthroposophical knowledge of Man and of the Cosmos in its spiritual essence; also what may be called 'anthroposophical history', told as an outcome of research into the spiritual world."

A brief list of anthroposophical literature will be found at the end of this volume, together with a summarised plan of the Complete Centenary Edition of Rudolf Steiner's works in the original German.

---

* The course consisted of 13 lectures, a revised translation of which is in preparation (1966).

ABOUT THE TRANSCRIPTS OF LECTURES

"The results of my anthroposophical work are, first, the books available to the general public; secondly, a great number of lecture-courses, originally regarded as private publications and sold only to members of the Theosophical (later Anthroposophical) Society. The courses consist of more or less accurate notes taken at my lectures, which for lack of time I have not been able to correct. I would have preferred the spoken word to remain the spoken word. But the members wished to have the courses printed for private circulation. Thus they came into existence. Had I been able to correct them the restriction: *for members only* would have been unnecessary from the beginning. As it is, the restriction was dropped more than a year ago.

In my autobiography it is especially necessary to say a word about how my books for the general public on the one hand, and the privately printed courses on the other, belong within what I elaborated as Anthroposophy.

Someone who wishes to trace my inner struggle and effort to present Anthroposophy in a way that is suitable for present-day consciousness must do so through the writings published for general distribution. In these I define my position in relation to the philosophical striving of the present. They contain what to my *spiritual sight* became ever more clearly defined, the edifice of Anthroposophy—certainly incomplete in many ways.

But another requirement arose, different from that of elaborating Anthroposophy and devoting myself solely to problems connected with imparting facts directly from the spiritual world to the general cultural life of today: the requirement of meeting fully the inner need and spiritual longing of the members.

Especially strong were the requests to have light thrown by Anthroposophy upon the Gospels and the Bible in general. The members wished to have courses of lectures on these revelations bestowed upon mankind.

In meeting this need through private lecture courses, another factor arose: at these lectures only members were present. They were familiar with basic content of Anthroposophy. I could address them as people advanced in anthroposophical knowledge. The approach I adopted in these lectures was not at all suitable for the written works intended primarily for the general public.

In these private circles I could formulate what I had to say in a way I should have been *obliged* to modify had it been planned initially for the general public.

Thus the public and the private publications are in fact two quite different things, built upon different foundations. The public writings are the direct result of my inner struggles and labours, whereas the privately printed material includes the inner struggle and labour of the members. I listened to the inner needs of the members, and my living experience of this determined the form of the lectures.

However, nothing was ever said that was not solely the result of my direct experience of the growing content of Anthroposophy. There was never any question of concessions to the prejudices or the preferences of the members. Whoever reads these privately-printed lectures can take them to represent Anthroposophy in the fullest sense. Thus it was possible without hesitation—when the complaints in this direction became too presistent—to depart from the custom of circulating this material only among members. But it must be borne in mind that faulty passages occur in these lecture-reports not revised by myself.

The right to judge such private material can of course, be conceded only to someone who has the pre-requisite basis for such judgment. And in respect of most of this material it would mean *at least* knowledge of man and of the cosmos insofar as these have been presented in the light of Anthroposophy, and also knowledge of what exists as 'anthroposophical history' in what has been imparted from the spiritual world."

Extract from *Rudolf Steiner, An Autobiography*, Chapter 35 pp. 386–388, 2nd Edition 1980, Steinerbooks, New York.

SUMMARY OF LECTURES

Lecture 1

Western world-views are concerned with man's place in the whole course of human history on Earth, whereas those of the East are content to envisage man in terms of *space* only. The essential nature of man can be seen in the evolution of his consciousness. Man experiences his own being in waking, dreaming and sleeping. In modern thinking he loses his real self. Descartes' *cogito ergo sum* is not based on something inwardly experienced but is only a convulsive effort to attach oneself to reality.

Remains of Druidic culture in Wales, near Penmaenmawr. Inner qualities of sunlight and the shadows it casts. The Druid priests and the stone circles. *Imaginations* are much more alive than abstract thoughts which can give no inkling of reality, but only pictures of it. Within the stone circles the Druid sought his science, his wisdom— his Sun-wisdom and also his Nature-wisdom. The actions and effects of the Sun and Moon on plant-life. Elemental beings and their activities. The good gods and their opponents. Medicinal properties of plants. Man's consciousness and disposition of soul were quite different when the Druid religion was in its prime—some three to five thousand years ago. Thinking was more dreamlike; when men woke they felt that something was still remaining over from sleep, like an 'after-taste'. They felt that they were received into a kind of grave by the forces of gravity. In certain souls —Boehme and Swedenborg are examples—something connected with evolution arises as a genuine memory of earlier times.

Stuttgart, 14th September, 1923

Lecture 2

In earlier periods of evolution, consciousness was filled more with living pictures than with abstract concepts. Elemental spirits were seen hovering around the plants. The activities of gigantic elemental beings in wind, frost and hail, storm and thunder. Men did not feel that their soul-life was separated from external Nature. Moreover they had an inner spiritual perception of the real being of man; they saw not only their present existence but their pre-earthly existence as well. But they came gradually to feel that the spirit had withdrawn from Nature, that they had been cast out of the spiritual world and thrust into a world to which, in their essential being, they did not belong. This mood expressed itself through the feeling that there had been a Fall of man. The Mysteries were the only source of consolation. Sleep was a draught of Nature, its aftermath being experienced as a kind of sweetness. In dreamless sleep man felt as though he was submerged in the Earth, as in a grave. Not only the forces of the Sun but also those of the Moon penetrate below the surface of the Earth. *The forces of the Moon work against the force of earthly gravity.* Man is drawn to the Earth by gravity and away from it by the forces of the Moon; for him as earthly man it is the Earth which has the upper hand. But as regards his head-activity, the effective influence on it is the *negative* gravity that draws him away. Thus though man might not be able to fly, at least he could raise his spirit into the starry spaces. Through this "astrological Initiation" men were taught by the Mystery-priests about the effects of the stellar environment upon them. Vision of Nature permeated by spirit became gradually clouded, but atavistic remains persisted. They manifest in sleep-walking, in men who are by nature "Sun-men" such as Jacob Boehme and Paracelsus, and in "Saturn-men" such as Swedenborg. The different character of seership in Boehme and Swedenborg.

Stuttgart, 15th September, 1923

Lecture 3   47

In earlier conditions of soul-life, man experienced his cosmic existence. Dreams and their characteristics. Every experience of which we have been aware must wait 3 or 4 days before it is fully our own, i.e. impressed upon the etheric and physical bodies—and then it is part, not of ourselves only, but also of the Cosmos. The meaning and purpose of the three days' sleep in the ancient form of Initiation. The laws we look for in the external world by our methods of observation and experiment cease to be valid inside the skin of a human being; the laws of the very substances consumed are changed, down to the smallest particles. "Our dreams are a protest against that part of reality which is shackled within the laws of Nature . . . the moment you enter, even to the slightest degree, into the spiritual world through your dreams, your dream-experience arises as a *protest against the laws of Nature.*" (Staudenmaier and the effects of mediumship upon him.) It is tragic for a modern man when he passes through Initiation to experience entry into a sphere of being where this protest against the laws of Nature is encountered; he feels that everything he had gained from his intellect, and which was determined by the laws of Nature, is swamped. But he finally realises that a different world—the *moral world-order*—is pressing in upon him. The vicarious Deed of Christ. Man was to take a step upwards in evolution and to experience in moral form what had previously come to him naturally. The Mystery of Golgotha is related closely to the meaning of earthly evolution because of its relation to the evolution of man's consciousness. We can visualise three states of consciousness: a dulled dream-life, waking life, and *a state of heightened waking consciousness*. Only through the latter can the Mystery of Golgotha be understood. In this present age of freedom we must resolve out of our own free knowledge to live on towards the goal laid down for us by the Divine Powers of the world.

Stuttgart, 16th September, 1923

Lecture 4

The Sun-Initiation of the Druid Priest and his Moon-Science

Cosmic processes in Earth-evolution. Sun Beings and Moon Beings; ancient memories of their existence and influence expressed in myths and sagas. Druid culture in its prime preceded the epoch of mythologies connected with the names of Wotan or Odin. Druid priests were the authorities by whom the whole life of the people was guided. Their wisdom was an unconscious memory of the Sun and Moon elements in the Earth before the separation of Sun and Moon. Initiation in the Druid Mysteries was a Sun-Initiation, bound up with Moon-wisdom. Cromlechs and dolmens: instruments whereby the *physical* effects of the Sun were shut off, enabling seers to observe the inner qualities of the Sun and the relation of the Earth to the Sun. Understanding of the Moon-forces which had remained in the Earth after the separation of the Moon. The Druid's science of Nature was a Moon-science. Giant elemental beings (Jötuns). Weather-processes and Earth-knowledge. Remedies, healing herbs. Wotan-Mercury. Runes. The Wotan impulse denotes the first entry of intellectualism. Wotan civilisation felt as an illness by Druidic culture. "Baldur ... the Sun-force coming from Wotan, is the Sun-force reflected back by Mercury." The death of Baldur and the Christ Impulse. Transition to abstract conceptions of medicine and remedies. The primeval wisdom once cultivated by the Moon Beings on the Earth was preserved through the Sun-Initiation of the Druid priests.

Dornach, 10th September, 1923

LECTURE 1

MAN IN THE PAST, THE PRESENT AND THE FUTURE

Stuttgart, 14th September 1923

For the subject of these lectures I have chosen an account of man's development during a particular period of the past, of his situation to-day, and of the outlook for his future evolution on this Earth-planet. No world-conception which has had any influence upon Western civilisation, or its American offshoot, has been content to deal only with present-day man and to show how the individual fits into the pattern of world-population. The world-conceptions acceptable to Western civilisation have always emphasised the place of man in the whole course of human history on Earth. They have always shown the relationship between man of the present and of the past, no matter whether they go back only to a certain point —as the Old Testament does in describing the history of the Earth—or whether they trace man right through the stages of cosmic evolution.

The philosophies of the East, and even the early philosophies of Europe, if they did not belong to our modern civilisation, were less concerned with this outlook. They were content to envisage man in terms of space only. The feeling we all have as a result of living within Western evolution makes it quite impossible for us to be satisfied with this spatial picture. There is a sort of psychological instinct in us to see ourselves in a brotherly association not only with men living to-day but also with men of the past; and unless we include both past and present we do not feel that we have a real notion of mankind.

But we can never have any satisfying idea of the historical

development of man, whether in a wider or in a narrower sense, if we are limited to the results of ordinary anthropology. Man is a being whose evolution we cannot comprehend with the aid of nothing but external documents, however brilliantly they may be interpreted. Man is a being of body, soul and spirit; he is a being who has been penetrated, to a lesser or greater extent, by the spirit, in such a way that consciousness has been alive within him. The whole nature and being of man can be seen in the development of his consciousness, just as the being of a plant is finally revealed to the senses in the flower.

Let us therefore go a little more deeply into this most vital aspect of human evolution—the evolution of consciousness. When we consider man's consciousness as it is to-day we can make certain distinctions. In our ordinary waking condition, as we know it from waking in the morning to the time of falling asleep, we develop a more or less clear and luminous life of ideas which grow out of our life of feeling as the flower grows out of the plant. Over against this clear and luminous life of ideas there is a further condition which never really becomes quite clear, but is more or less unconscious, dark, inwardly surging and weaving. Even deeper than the feelings, which do, after all, quite directly stimulate our life of thought and ideas—much deeper within our being there is our surging will. And I have often described to anthroposophists how in his *willing* man is, strictly speaking, asleep, even during his waking state. We never experience, in the waking conditions of our present-day consciousness, what lives within our willing. We have an idea that we are going to do this or that, but in this there is as yet no willing—only the intention to will clothed in the idea. Then the intention plunges into the depths of the human being, of which his consciousness has no clearer idea than it has of dreamless sleep. It then emerges as the will seen in the action of our arms and hands, legs and feet; in the activity we exercise on objects in the external world. Whenever we act thus through the will on our own body,

or in order to effect some change in the external world, we
become aware of it through our ideas—ideas which also have
some quality of feeling. Our ordinary consciousness perceives
only the beginning and the end of willing, the intention in the
form of an idea, and then again, also in the form of an idea,
the consciousness observes our own movements or those in the
external world which arise out of these intentions. All that
lies between—how our intentions transfer themselves, via the
soul, into our organism, how the soul arouses the physical
warmth, the movement of the blood and muscles which then
produce an act of will—of all this we are as unaware as we
are of the events in dreamless sleep.

If we really manage to observe what happens, we must say
that we are actually awake only in our ideas (our conceptual
life); we dream in our feelings and sleep in our willing. Our
knowledge of this willing is just like the experience of waking
in the morning and noticing that our organism has somehow
recuperated and refreshed itself. We perceive the effects of
sleep when we wake. Similarly, we have the intention to
perform some act of will; we transmit it unconsciously into
our organism where, as though in sleep, it passes over into
activity and deed; and we wake up again only with our action
and see the result of what has been going on within us, of
which we have been quite unconscious.

Such in broad outline is man's experience of his own being
in waking, dreaming and sleeping. After all, the dreams we
have when we are sleeping have very little relation to our
ideas. They obey quite other laws than the logical laws of our
conceptual life. But if we observe things closely we shall see
that the course of our dreaming, with its marvellous dramatic
quality that is so often typical of dreams, bears an extraordinarily close resemblance to our life of feeling. If in our
waking life we were capable only of feeling, those feelings
would not, it is true, be very like the pictures of our dreams.
But the dramatic quality, tensions, impulsive wishes and crises
of the inner life, with their turmoil of emotion, are displayed

in our feelings just as vaguely—or if you like, just as indefin-
itely—as they are in our dreams; with this difference, that
the basis of a dream lies in its pictures, whereas our feelings
live in those peculiar experiences which we describe in terms
of our inner life. Thus in the present state of human consciousness we may include our feelings and actual dreaming as part
of the dream-state, and in the same way include our willing
and actual dreamless sleep as part of the sleeping state.

We must, however, realise that what we are now describing
as the basic quality of our present-day consciousness has
passed through a process of evolution in a comparatively
recent period, though we do not like taking much notice of
this in our materialistic age. But you will not understand the
surviving documents of human thought, even of the early
Christian centuries, unless you realise that the inner activity of
men in those days was quite different from what lives within
our souls to-day as the activity of thought. In particular it
would be a complete psychological error to seek to understand Scotus Erigena's work, "On the Parts of Nature" (*De
Divisione Naturae*), written in the ninth century, for example,
or the older writings on alchemy, with the conceptual intellect
which has become normal to-day. We simply cannot understand what they were driving at if our modern type of thinking is employed. We can read the words, but we shall not
grasp the meaning.

Human thinking since the fifteenth century has acquired a
particular character which may have developed only slowly
but has more or less already reached its culminating point.
Yet this way of thinking, which represents the actual waking
condition for modern man, is not really capable of giving him
any satisfaction. A man can think, and that is the only
luminous experience of his waking life. He can think, and
that is the only means by which he can draw on his inner
powers and establish the marvellous results of the sciences.
Yet basically this modern thinking can give man no satisfaction for his inner yearnings. The fact is that he loses his

own self in this modern thought. He does of course experience this thinking as the one clear element in his consciousness—much clearer, for instance, than his breathing or blood circulation, which remain obscure in the deeper regions of his consciousness. He feels that these also may contain some reality, but he sleeps through this reality, and it is only in his ideas and thinking that he is awake. But then, especially if he is disposed to a certain amount of self-observation, he comes to feel that although it is only in his thinking that he fulfils his inner being, yet his true self is lost. And I can give you two examples which will enable you—spiritually of course—to lay hands on this loss of self in thought.

There is a famous philosopher of modern times, *Descartes*, who is the originator of the famous saying, *cogito ergo sum*—I think, therefore I am. So this philosopher says. But to-day men do not and cannot say it. For when we merely think something or experience it in thinking, it does not follow that it "is", nor that I "am" merely because I myself am thinking. For us these thoughts are at most pictures; they may be the most certain thing in us, but we do not grasp any "being" through our thinking. Again, we often say that if we think something, that is "nothing but thinking". So also in Descartes' case: he wants to "be" and cannot find any other point at which to grasp this "being" of man, and so he seeks it where the common man certainly does not feel it to be—in thought. We do not *think* in sleep, but does it follow then that we *are* not? Do we die in the evening and are we reborn each morning? Or do we exist between falling asleep and waking? The simplest truths are in fact not taken into account by present-day views of the world. Descartes' "I think, therefore I am" is not based on something inwardly experienced, but is only a convulsive effort to attach oneself to reality. That is the first point.

The second point I want to make is this. Besides his thinking, of which modern man is very proud, we have the results of natural science, results of observation or experiment. In point of fact these do not help us to see the real being of things, but only the changes that occur in them—that which is transitory. And nowadays people consider a thought to be justified only if it derives from this external actuality, which after all reveals only a manifestation of itself. So we have ceased completely to grasp our real "being" in ourselves; our thought is too much in the air. We have no way of finding anything else in us except by methods that science applies to Nature; and then we seek our real being in that. In consequence, man to-day believes only in that part of himself which is part of Nature. Nature and the form of existence associated with it thus become a sort of Moloch which robs modern man of any real feeling of his own being.

Many people will perhaps retort that they don't notice anything of the sort, and will contradict what I have said. But that is only their opinion. The feelings which modern men have, at least if they have even the elements of self-awareness, are the outcome of the mood I have just described. They are encased, as it were, within this experience of their own being and their relation to the external world, and they then transfer the consequence of this condition to their consciousness of the world. For instance, they may observe the stars with their telescopes, spectroscopes and other instruments. They record what these instruments show and then build up a purely spatial astronomy and astrophysics. They do not notice that they are merely transferring to the heavens what they have observed and calculated about things on the Earth.

Thus, suppose that I have here some source of light. We all admit that if I move thousands of miles away from it, the light will become weaker and perhaps no longer visible. We all know that the strength of the light decreases with distance. Ordinary physics states the law that gravitation, too, decreases with the square of the distance. But people don't pursue this thought further. They can demonstrate that here on Earth, gravity has a particular magnitude and diminishes with the square of the distance, for they live on the Earth and establish laws of Nature and truths valid for the Earth, and build them into a system. Where gravity has a definite magnitude, these laws are true. The force of gravity decreases, but so does truth. What was true for the Earth ceases to be true if we pursue it further outwards into the Universe. We have no more right to regard the findings of physics and chemistry as applicable to the whole Universe than we have to assume that earthly gravity holds good throughout the Cosmos. The truths that rule in the heavenly spheres cannot be dealt with in the same way as those that hold on Earth. Of course to say this sort of thing nowadays is considered highly paradoxical —even crazy. But our general consciousness is so solidly encased nowadays that even the slightest remark which might pierce through the case immediately appears strange. Modern men are so wholly tied to the Earth that their knowledge, even sometimes their reflections, never pass beyond what they experience on Earth. And they deal with cosmic time exactly as they deal with cosmic space.

I was particularly impressed with all this recently. (I have often discussed this sort of truth among anthroposophists and what I am saying now is only a repetition based on a particular example.) This struck me with particular force when I was invited by our English anthroposophical friends to give a course of lectures at Penmaenmawr in the second half of August.* Penmaenmawr is in Wales, where the island of Anglesey lies over against the West coast of Britain. It is really an extraordinary region which shows that there are quite different geographies over the Earth's surface from those you will find discussed in textbooks, even for the most advanced students. Ordinarily we think it more than enough if a

* *The Evolution of the World and of Humanity.* 13 lectures, 19th–31st August, 1923. (Revised edition in preparation, 1966.) The title of the German text in the Complete Centenary Edition is: *Initiations-Erkenntnis. Die geistige und physische Welt- und Menschheitsentwicklung in der Vergangenheit, Gegenwart und Zukunft vom Gesichtspunkte der Anthroposophie.*

geographical description includes the character of the vegetation, flora and fauna, and if in addition we base it on the geological and palaeontological nature of the region. But the Earth displays differentiations of a much more inward nature than any you will ordinarily find in geographical works. Thus in Penmaenmawr, where these lectures were held, you have only to go a short distance, a mile or so into the mountains, and all over the place you can find the remains of the old Druid cults, fallen stone circles of a simple sort. For instance, stones are put together to enclose a small space and covered with another stone so as to form a little chamber, where the light of the sun could be cut off, leaving the chamber in darkness. I do not dispute that such cromlechs had also to serve as burial places, for at all times the most important centres of worship have been set up over the graves of fellow-men. But here, even with these simple cromlechs, we have something further, as is indeed indicated by the so-called Druid circles.

It was a wonderful experience when I went with a friend one day to one of these mountains at Penmaenmawr, on which the scanty remains of two such circles are still to be seen lying very close to each other. Even to-day it can be seen from the position of the stones that there were once twelve of them, and if one wants to discover their purpose they must be observed closely. Now while the sun follows his course through the Cosmos, whether during a day or during a year, a quite specific shadow is cast beneath each stone; and the path of the sun could be traced by following the shadow as it changed in the course of a day or year. We are still sensitive to light to-day, especially if light is associated with warmth or warmth with light. Present-day consciousness can naturally also notice the difference between the light of the summer and winter sun, since we are warm in summer and cold in winter; and we may note finer differences too. But, you see, the same differences we can notice in so obvious a fashion in the light, when we are either warm or freezing, can be per-

ceived in the shadow as well. There is a difference between
the October sun and the July or August sun, not only in the
direction but in the *quality* of the shadow. One of the duties
of the Druids was to develop a special faculty for perceiving
the quality of the shadow—for perceiving, let us say, the
peculiar intermingling of a red tone in the August shadow or
of a blue one in that of November or December. Thus the
Druids were able, by the training they received, to read off
the daily and yearly course of the sun in the shadows. We can
still see from these remains that one of the tasks they under-
took was something of this sort. There were many other things
that belonged to this cult : a Sun ritual, which, however, was
not a mere abstraction, not even the abstraction we see in
devotion and reverence. Without undervaluing devotion and
reverence, it would be a complete error to believe that. But
devotion and reverence were not in this case the essentials, for
the cult included something quite different.

Take the grain of wheat or rye. It must be planted within
the Earth at a particular moment of the year, and it is a bad
thing for it to be planted at an inappropriate moment. Anyone who has exact knowledge of these things is well aware
that it makes a difference whether a seed is planted a few
days earlier or later. There are other things of this sort in
human life. The people who lived about three thousand years
ago in the region where the Druid cult flourished led an
extremely simple life. Agriculture and cattle-raising were the
chief occupations. But we may ask how they were to know
when to sow and harvest in the best way, or when they were
to attend to the many other jobs which Nature requires in the
course of a year. Nowadays of course we have farmers'
calendars which tell the farmer that on such and such a day
such and such a job needs to be done, and tell him very
intelligently. In our day, with our type of consciousness, this
information can be catalogued and read off from the printed
page. We think nothing of it, but the fact remains that there
was none of that, not even the most primitive form of reading

and writing, in the days when the Druid religion was in its prime. On the other hand, the Druids could stand in one of these stone circles and by observing the shadow they could proclaim, for instance, that during the next week farmers must undertake this or that work, or the bulls be introduced to the herd since the moment was right for the mating of the cows. The Druids were equipped to read in the Cosmos; they used the signs produced by those monuments of which we have to-day only such scanty remains, and could read from them the information the sun gave them of what was to be done on Earth.

The constitution of the soul was in fact quite different, and it would be a serious conceit on our part if, just because we are capable of this little bit of reading and writing, we were to undervalue the art which made it possible to lay down the work and activities required on Earth through these revelations of the heavens. In places like Penmaenmawr we are impelled to recollect many other things, too, which Spiritual Science is peculiarly qualified to investigate.

I have often pointed out in anthroposophical circles how ordinary thoughts are inadequate to grasp what Spiritual Science can investigate and how we have to conceive it in Imaginations. I assume you all know what I have said about Imaginations in my book *Knowledge of the Higher World and its Attainment*. It is these Imaginations and not our ordinary ideas which we must have in our souls when we are describing things on the basis of some immediate spiritual observation and not of external sense-perception. The genuinely spiritual-scientific accounts which are given you in our anthoposophical lectures have their origin in Imaginations of that kind.

Now these Imaginations are much more alive than ordinary abstract thoughts, which can give us no inkling of what reality is, but only pictures of it. Imaginations on the other hand, can be laid hold of by active thinking, in the same way that we can grasp tables and chairs. We are much more vigorously permeated by reality when our knowledge comes from Imaginations and not from abstract concepts. Anyone who speaks on the basis of Imaginations always has them before him as though he were writing something down— writing, however, not with those terribly abstract signs which constitute our writing, but with cosmic pictures.

Now what is the position with regard to these Imaginations in our district here? Anyone who knows them knows also that it is pretty easy to attain them, pretty easy to form them. If he has a sense of responsibility when describing anything through Spiritual Science, he will allow these Imaginations to take effect—that is, to inscribe them in the spirit—only when he has pondered them a good deal and tested them thoroughly. Nobody who speaks out of the spiritual world with a full sense of responsibility has a facile tongue. Nevertheless we can say that in districts like ours here it is relatively easy to inscribe these Imaginations, but they are obliterated equally easily. If in districts like this we create a spiritual content in Imaginations—I cannot put it in any other way— we find it is like writing something down and immediately afterwards rubbing it out. But there in Wales, where land and sea meet and the tides ebb and flow each day, where the wind blows through and through you—for instance in the hotel where we were staying you could not only feel the wind blowing in at the windows, but when one walked on the carpet it was like walking on a rough sea because of the wind blowing under the carpet—where moreover Nature is so full of life and so joyful in its life that you may get almost hourly alternations of rain and sunshine, then you do really come to see how Nature revealed herself to the Druid priests—or I might say the learned Druids, for it would be the same thing—when they gazed upon her from their mountain height. How then did the Earth appear to the Druid's spiritual eye when the heavens had the character I have just described?

This is very interesting to observe, though you will only

realise it fully if you can grasp the particular geographical quality of the place. There you have to exert yourself much more vigorously if you want to construct Imaginations than you do, for instance, here. There, they are much more difficult to inscribe in the astral atmosphere. On the other hand they are more permanent and are not so easily extinguished. You come to realise how these old Druids chose for their most important cult-centres, just such places in which the spiritual, as it approaches mankind, expresses itself to some extent in the quality of the place. Those Druid circles we visited—well, if we had gone up in a balloon and looked down from above on the larger and the smaller circles, for though they are some distance apart you would not notice that when you are a certain height above them—the circles would have appeared like the ground-plan of the Goetheanum which has been destroyed by fire. It is a wonderfully situated spot! As you climb the heights, you have wide views over land and sea. Then you reach the top and the Druid circles lie before you —there where the hill is hollowed out, so that you find yourself in a ring of hills, and within this ring of hills are the Druid circles. It was there that the Druid sought his science, his knowledge, his wisdom; there that he sought his Sun-wisdom but also his Nature-wisdom.

As the Druid penetrated into the relationship between what he saw on Earth and what streamed down from the heavens, he saw the whole processes of plant-growth and vegetation quite differently from the way in which they appear to our abstract thought of later days. If we can properly grasp the true quality of the sun, on the one hand the physical rays which enter our eyes, on the other the shadow with its various gradations, we come to realise that the *spiritual* essence of the sun lives on in the various grades of shadow. The shadow prevents only the physical rays of the sun from reaching other bodies, whereas the spiritual penetrates further. In the cromlechs which I have described to you, a small dark place is separated off. But it is only the physical sunlight which cannot penetrate there; its *activity* penetrates, and the Druid, as gradually through this activity he came to be permeated by the secret forces of cosmic existence, entered into the secrets of the world. Thus, for instance, the actions of the sun on plants was revealed to him; he could see that a particular kind of plant-life flourishes at a particular time when the sun is active in a particular way. He could trace the spiritual activity of the sun and see how it pours and streams into flower, leaf and root; and it was the same with animals. And while he was thus able inwardly to recognise the activity of the sun, he also began to see how other activities from the Cosmos, for example, those of the moon, pour into it. He could see that the effect of the sun was to promote sprouting growth, with an upward tendency, and so he knew that if a plant as it grows out from the soil were exposed only to the sun, it would grow unendingly. The sun brings forth burgeoning, luxuriant life. If this life is checked and reduced to form, if leaves, blossom, seed and fruit assume a specific shape, if what strives towards the infinite is variously limited—all this has its origin in the activities of the moon. And these are to be found not only in the reflected light of the sun, for the moon reflects all influences, and these in their turn can be seen in the growth of the plant out of its root and also in what lives in the propagation of animals, and so on.

Let us take a particular instance. The Druid observed the growing plant; he observed in a more living way what, later on, Goethe observed more abstractly in his idea of metamorphosis. The Druid saw the downward streaming sun-forces, but he saw also the *reflected* sun-forces in everything that gives the plant its form. In his natural science he saw the combined activity of sun and moon in every single plant and animal. He could perceive the action of sun and moon on the root, which is wholly within the Earth and has the function of absorbing the salts of the Earth in a particular way. He could see that the action of sun and moon was quite different on the leaf, which wrests itself out of the Earth and presses forward into the air. Again, he saw a different action on the flower, which pushes onwards to the light of the sun. He could see as a unity the activity of the sun and moon, mediated by the activity of the Earth; to him, plant-growth and the being of the animal were also a unity.

Of course his life there was just what we experienced, with the winds raging around, which can reveal so much about the structure of the region, with the peculiar weather conditions which manifest themselves so vividly in that district. Thus, for example, at the beginning of one of our Eurythmy performances, which took place in a wooden hall, the audience sat with their umbrellas up, because just before the performance there had been a heavy downpour which was still going on when the performance began. The curtains were quite wet! This intimate association with Nature which can still be experienced to-day was of course also experienced by the Druids. Nature there is not so hard; she almost embraces one. It really is a delightful experience. I might almost say that one is drawn on and accompanied by the activity of Nature; one seems to be part of it. I even met people who maintained that one need not really eat there, that one can be fed by this very activity of Nature.

The Druid, then, lived with his Sun-Initiation within this activity of Nature, and he saw as the unity I have described the sun and moon mediated through the activity of the Earth, the growth of the plant, the growth of root, leaf and flower; and all this not in the form of abstract laws as to-day, but of living elemental beings. Different elemental beings of sun and moon were active in the root, in the leaf and in the flower. He could also pursue in the wider realms of Nature what is so beneficially differentiated in root, leaf and flower. Through his imaginative gifts he could see the small elemental beings restricted to narrow limits in the root, and he knew that what lives in beneficial form in the root can free itself and expand to the gigantic. Thus he saw the large-scale activities of Nature as the small activities of the plant raised to a gigantic power. Just as he had spoken of the elemental beings in the root of the plant, he could also speak of these root-beings as having expanded in a cosmically irregular way and manifesting in the formation of frost, dew and hail. On the one hand he spoke of the root-beings who were beneficially active, and of the giants of frost and ice which are these root-beings grown to gigantic size.

Again, he spoke of the elemental activities in the leaf of the plant, which permeate themselves with the forces of the air; he traced them into the distant spaces of Nature, and he then saw that, if what lives in the leaf frees itself and strives beyond its proper limits into the distances of Nature, it manifests in the surging of winds. The giants of wind and storm are the elemental beings of the plant grown beyond their size. And the element which is distilled in the flower and meets the sunlight, and produces in the flower the etheric oils with their phosphoric quality—if that is freed, it manifests itself as the giants of fire, among whom, for instance, Loki belongs. In this science of sun and moon, therefore, the Druid saw as a unity both that which lives in the narrowly restricted space of the plant and that which frees itself and lives in wind and weather.

But he went further. He said to himself : When that which lives in root, leaf and flower is contained within the desirable limits set by the good gods, normal plant-growth results. If it appears in hoar frost, that is the work of opposing beings : for the elemental beings, growing into powers of opposition, create the harmful, devastating aspects of Nature. Now as a human being I can make use of the devastating activities of the beings who are the opponents of the gods; I can gather the hoar frost in appropriate ways, and the products of the storm and whatever is caught up in the surging of wind and rain. I can make use of the giant forces for my own purposes by burning the plant, for instance, and reducing it to ashes, to charcoal and so on. I can take these forces, and by using frost, hail and rain and other such things, or what the giants of fire control—things which are the expression of forces that have grown to harmful vastness—I can protect the normal growth of the plant. I can rob these giants of all this and can treat normal plants with it, and by applying these forces of the opposing powers I can make healing medicines out of the good elemental forces which have remained within their proper limits. And this was in fact one of the ways of making medicines out of plants, by employing frost and snow and ice and by the use of burning and calcination. The Druid felt it to be his work to take whatever was harmful from the opposing giant powers and restore it to the service of the good gods. We can trace these things in many different ways.

Now why am I spending time on this? I want to use it as an example—and I quote this particular one because I do indeed think that the Penmaenmawr lecture-course was a very important event in the history of the Anthroposophical Movement—to show how man's consciousness and his whole constitution of soul were quite different at a time not so very far removed from the present. With his present-day consciousness man cannot realise what lived in the consciousness of this ancient humanity. And what I have said of that ancient humanity could also be said of other peoples. There we catch glimpses of a quite different constitution of soul. Men in those days had no idea of what we experience as abstract thoughts. All their thinking was more dreamlike, and they did not live within such sharply outlined ideas and concepts as we do to-day. They lived in dreams which were much more vivid and alive, more full of substance; and indeed their waking life was really a sort of continuation of their dreaming. Just as nowadays we live in an alternation of dreaming or dreamless sleep and the abstract ideas of our waking life, so they alternated between this dreamlike everyday life and a dreamless sleep which was not wholly like ours. When they woke they felt that there was still something remaining over from sleep—something which afforded a sort of nourishment for the soul, which they had absorbed during sleep and which could still be felt, indeed could still be "tasted". In those days men felt the after-taste of sleep in their whole organism. There was a third condition which no longer occurs in human consciousness, a feeling of being surrounded by the Earth, and when a man woke up he felt not only that he had been asleep—of which he retained an after-taste—but that he had been received into a kind of grave by the forces of gravity, that gravity had closed him in, and he was, as it were, within the embrace of the Earth.

Now just as we can describe our present-day states of consciousness as waking, dreaming and sleeping, so we should have to say that at a certain stage of the past there were the three states of dreaming, sleeping and being surrounded by the Earth. Since everything which evolves in the course of history has some sort of relation to the present, we find human souls in whom, during a later earth-life something peculiar appears, like a genuine memory of earlier times, something connected with their earlier earth-life. Men like this display what for their own age is abnormal, but which is a living memory of their souls. Examples of this were Jacob Boehme and Swedenborg, and in such spirits something connected with human evolution lights up into contemporary humanity from a very distant past.

To-morrow I will say more about the special qualities of vision in Boehme and Swedenborg; this will help us to understand the past of humanity and also the three future states of consciousness.

LECTURE 2

MAN IN THE PAST, THE PRESENT AND THE FUTURE

Stuttgart, 15th September 1923

Yesterday I used the culture of the Druids—which at the moment is particularly relevant to the development of our Anthroposophical Movement—to illustrate the soul-quality of an earlier age in a particular region. If we go back three or four or five thousand years—it varies in different parts of the Earth—we can always penetrate into a quite different type of soul-quality, and we then find that the whole spiritual and social guidance of human life in a particular period follows the pattern laid down by such a quality. The development to which I am referring is connected with the gradual evolution of human consciousness. It would be true to say that in olden times men were quite different beings from what they are to-day, and in the future they will again be different. Ordinary history tells little of this and so as soon as we get a few centuries away from the present, ordinary history, as it is presented to us, is to a considerable extent quite illusory as an aid to a real understanding of man.

In the lecture yesterday I pointed out how we should have to study three main stages of human consciousness, though naturally with many different shadings. The states of consciousness with which we are familiar—waking, dreaming and sleeping—are valid only for the present—which may extend over hundreds or even thousands of years, yet from an historical point of view is still the present. If we go back into older periods of human evolution we no longer find the sort of waking condition of to-day, with its logically interrelated concepts. The farther we go back, the more do we fail to find this logical consciousness, which appeared in full development only during the fourteenth and fifteenth centuries, though it had begun in the later period of Greek culture. In earlier times, on the other hand, we discover a type of consciousness filled much more with living pictures than with abstract concepts; and we find this consciousness in man everywhere.

Natural forces in our sense were quite unknown to an older humanity. In the times I spoke of yesterday, people did not talk of meteorological laws controlling wind and weather, but, as I explained, of *beings* seen pictorially, of elemental spirits hovering around the plants, or of gigantic spiritual beings active in wind and weather, frost and hail, storm and thunder. All this was living in their observation of Nature without any logical deductions. Everything they saw, including the phenomena of Nature, was a living, weaving, surging of spiritual beings. The whole basis of their inner condition of soul was quite different from ours.

In a sense, men were more self-enclosed, but in a way very different from what we know to-day; this living in themselves was at the same time a consciousness full of living dream-pictures which led them out into the distant spaces of the Cosmos. Men saw pictures, though not in the way in which to-day we have thoughts, when the things are outside. While they had these experiences of the giants of frost, storm and fire, of the spirits of root, leaf and flower, they felt themselves united with plant, root, leaf, flower, with thunder and with lightning. Because they experienced the spiritual and spiritual pictures in their own being, they did not therefore feel their soul-life separated from external Nature.

If not in the very oldest periods described in my book *Occult Science*, at least in those that followed them, one can observe spiritually how this constitution of soul was accompanied by a general mood in the peoples who at the time were the most civilised. There was a time when men had an inner spiritual perception of the real being of man. In these pictures I have just spoken of they saw not only their present existence but their pre-earthly existence as well; just as we can see a perspective of space, they saw a perspective of *time*. It was not a recollection but an actual seeing; and they saw beyond their birth into a spiritual world from which they had descended into the life of man on Earth. It was quite natural for a member of this older humanity to see into his pre-earthly existence and to feel : I am a spiritual being, since before I assumed this earthly body I rested in the bosom of the spirit and spent my time within it, and there experienced my human destiny—not yet in a physical body but—if I may say so, however paradoxical it may sound—in a spiritual body.

To demand that one should believe in the spirit would have been absurd for this older humanity just as it is absurd to ask modern men to believe in mountains; you don't believe in them, you see them. In those days men saw their pre-natal spiritual life, though of course they saw it with the eyes of the soul. But there came a time when they indeed saw spiritually this inner being of man as the outcome of pre-earthly existence, while external Nature surrounding them became increasingly a sort of riddle. Pure sense-perception made its way gradually into human evolution. In very early times, such as those of ancient India, as I described them in *Occult Science,* men still saw everything, Nature included, spiritually. It marked a step forward when the vision of the spiritual remained inward, but Nature, if I may put it so, became gradually de-spiritualised. While man still felt inwardly that he was spirit born of spirit, when he looked outward to the blossoming of Nature, to the clouds from which the lightning flashes, to the wind and weather, to the delicate, wonderfully formed crystals, to hill and dale, a mood came over him which can be traced by Spiritual Science over long periods, especially over the times when men were civilised. They might have expressed it as follows : We men are spirit born of spirit; in our pre-earthly existence our being was knit together with the spiritual, but now we are transplanted into the environment of Nature. We behold the lovely flowers, the vast mountains, the mighty power of Nature in wind and weather, but the spirit is withdrawn.

Thus the notion of a purely material Nature in the environment increasingly arose. Men felt—I mean of course those who were the most developed, the men whom we should call civilised in our modern sense—they saw that their body was formed out of the substances of this Nature which for them had lost its divine-spiritual quality. If men nowadays felt anything like this, they would begin to think, to speculate and philosophise about it. It was not so with the men of that earlier time. Without reflection they experienced a great disharmony within themselves : "I come as spirit from a world of spirit, my essential being has descended from divine heights, but I am clothed with substance taken from a Nature which the spirit seems to have abandoned; my spiritual existence is interwoven with something that does not reveal the spirit. My body is made up out of the same substances as the flowers of the field and the water of the clouds and rain, but these substances have lost their divine quality."

Those men felt as if they had been expelled from the spiritual world and thrust into a world to which in their essential being they did not really belong. It was of course possible to reject or to sleep through this mood, as happens nowadays with various aspects of our civilisation. But those who were awake at that time felt it, and it is through moods and feelings like this and not in thoughts and concepts that mankind develops.

Even the way in which our thoughts evolve nowadays is only an episode—as indeed these lectures will show—and anyone who speaks merely in the form of thoughts is speaking in an unreal way. This is particularly true of the way we speak nowadays. The people who pride themselves most on being practical and are filled with conceit about it are basically the worst theorists. We have these theorists in offices, in schools—obviously in schools, but no less in offices and commercial houses—and everything there has a theoretical bias and thoughts run riot. But it is only an episode without any essential truth. These people will attain to some truth in their thinking about life only if they feel once more as men did when they found Nature de-spiritualised, when they feel that they are an outcast race, taken from a divine-spiritual world where they really belong, into one where their inmost human being is a stranger.

One of the ways in which this mood expressed itself was through the feeling that there had been a Fall of man.* This idea arose from a change that had come about in human consciousness. Men felt that they had been thrust out of a spiritual world and that the reason for this must lie in some original sin. Thus at a particular epoch the conception of original sin, of the Fall of man, dawned in human consciousness.

If we understand the changes in human consciousness from the past through the present into the future, we shall also be able to understand how this conception of original sin, of a pre-historic Fall of man, arose. And at the same time when this mood came over man, his need was not for some grey theory, but for words through which souls needing comfort could find healing power. And what we have often described as the guidance of mankind in the old centres of ritual and religion, in the Mysteries, can be seen arising at a particular period of time coinciding approximately with ancient Persian and the earliest Chaldean culture in the Near East—it can be seen to coincide with what came from the priests, the great comforters of mankind. Consolation streamed from them and the Mysteries they celebrated; and indeed, human consciousness at that time was greatly in need of consolation. The words of the Mysteries had to contain some quality of soul that could speak to men's hearts with a power of healing and consolation. This is the epoch which exhibited such magnifi-

* See *The Mystery of the Trinity*, 4 lectures given in Dornach, 23rd–30th July, 1923; also, *Concepts of Original Sin and Grace*, lecture given in Munich, 3rd May, 1911.

cent creative power (though in a somewhat different form from later periods) in the spheres of art and religion, and a great deal in our art and in our religious ideas derives from that time, particularly the symbols, pictures and ritualistic ceremonies.

What was the source from which these teachers of the Mysteries drew in order to give this consolation? If the general waking consciousness consisted in the sort of living picture-consciousness I have described, yet at that time too there were three stages of consciousness. Nowadays we have sleeping, dreaming and waking. In those days, as opposed to the waking dream which, as I showed yesterday, was the normal form of waking consciousness, sleep was not as it is to-day, when it completely damps down our consciousness. Although with those men, too, consciousness was dimmed during sleep, there remained something of it on waking. Yesterday I described this by saying that when men woke after sleep they had a sort of after-taste. Most people felt, not merely on the tongue or in the mouth, deeply permeated by a certain sweetness of experience which was the after-taste of their sleep. This sweetness they experienced in sleep spread over from their life of sleep into that of waking. This sweetness was to them a test of the healthiness of their life, whereas if other tastes were present it was evidence of illness.

It sounds strange to say that an older humanity experienced the sweet after-effects of sleep in the limbs, the arms, right down into the finger-tips and the other members. But spiritual-scientific investigation shows that it was so; and the genius of language has retained something of this, though in a crude and materialised form. A sleeping-draught was once something spiritual : that is, sleep itself, and it was only later that it became an actual liquid draught in a material form. Sleep was then itself a draught of Nature, which extinguished the ordinary memories of day; it was a draught of forgetfulness. What ordinary men had from it was only a vague after-feeling, but Initiation gave the Mystery teachers, who were the leaders of humanity, a more exact consciousness of what really was experienced in sleep. In modern Initiation we ascend from our ordinary ideas to spirit-sight, but in those days, while ordinary men passed from their dream-waking life into sleep, for which they cultivated a consciousness and experienced this after-taste, the Mystery priests had means to feel their way consciously into sleep and so got to know what this after-taste implied. They learned of the water beyond physical existence, the water into which the human soul plunged during sleep each night—the waters of the weaving astrality of the world.

But that was only a second condition beyond the waking and dreaming of ordinary life. The third condition was one of which modern humanity has no knowledge at all, a condition deeper than dreamless sleep to-day. I said yesterday that one might call it a state of being surrounded by the Earth, and this was the condition of man at night during deep sleep. Only the priest of the Mysteries by means of his Initiation could attain consciousness of it and impart the results of this experience, which constituted the knowledge of those days. Men felt themselves embraced by the Earth, but they felt something more; they felt that in the ordinary course of the day they had come into a condition very near death, a death, however, from which there was an awakening. They experienced this third condition of consciousness as if they had actually descended into the Earth and been laid in a grave, yet not one that could be called an earthly grave. I will try to make clear to you in the following way how this grave not only was, but *how* it had to be, conceived.

Now when the Sun's rays fall on to the Earth, they are not merely reflected from flowers and stars. Farmers know this better than the city dweller does, for during the winter they use the Sun's warmth which has penetrated into the Earth. At that time of the year we have within the Earth what has streamed into it during the summer. Not only the Sun's warmth but other forces stream into the Earth. Yet from the point of view of which I am speaking this was the less important fact; the more important was that the activities of the *Moon* could also penetrate below the surface of the Earth to a certain extent. It was a pleasant idea of those days, not just a poetical idea but, in a way, a super-poetical one—though of course not held in any logical conception as we should to-day, but as a picture—when men thought of the light of the Sun streaming down to Earth in the light of the full Moon and penetrating a certain distance into the Earth, then being reflected not just from the Earth's surface but from its interior, after the light had been absorbed by the Earth.

The silver ebb and flow of the moonlight were experienced by man as the rhythmic play of its rays. It was not only a beautiful picture; the priests of the Mysteries knew something definite about this flowing moonlight. They knew that man is subject to gravitation as he lives on the Earth; that gravity holds him to the surface of the Earth, and thus the Earth draws his being to itself, as it were. The forces of the Moon were known to work against this force of gravity. They are in general weaker than the vigorous forces of the Earth's gravity, but they work against those forces. It was known that man is not just a clod held fast by the Earth's gravity but that he is rather in a sort of balance, drawn to the Earth by gravity and away from it by the forces of the Moon, and that for him as earthly man it is the Earth which holds the upper hand. But as regards his head-activity, the effective influence on it is the negative gravity that draws him away. Thus though man might not be able to fly, at least he could raise his spirit into the starry spaces. By means of this Initiation, through these Moon activities, humanity in those days learnt from their Mystery-priests the effect on earthly man of his starry environment.

This was the astrological Initiation, so much abused nowadays, which was specially prevalent among the people of ancient Chaldea. By its path men could learn not only of the activity of the Moon, but of that of the Sun, Mars,

Saturn, and so forth. Nowadays man is—if you will pardon a pictorial way of putting it so, for it is hard to describe such things in strictly logical words—man, as far as his knowledge goes, has become a kind of worm, not even an earthworm but something worse, a worm for whom it never rains so that he never emerges from the soil! Worms do after all emerge periodically when it rains, and then they can enjoy whatever is happening on the Earth's surface: and that is healthy for them. Modern man, with regard to his soul and spirit, is a worm for whom it never rains, and he is entirely encased in the Earth. Thus he believes that the members of his body grow on Earth more or less as stones are formed. He has no idea that the hair on his head is the result of the Sun's activity, for he is a worm which never comes above ground, a creature, that is, which bears the Sun-forces within him but never comes to the surface to investigate them. As the old Mystery-priests well knew, man has not grown out of the Earth like a cabbage; he has been created by the joint activity of the whole cosmic environment. You can see, therefore, how men in those days felt towards their Initiates and Mystery-leaders who could tell them from their training what his cosmic environment signifies for man.

These priests of the Mysteries could thus proclaim something which I shall have to give in an unimaginative form, since we are not nowadays capable of speaking as they did; they clothed all they said in wonderful poetry. The genius of language made that possible then, but nowadays we can no longer speak in such a way, because language is inadequate. If we had to put into words the message of the priests of the Mysteries to their people who came to them for comfort, feeling themselves thrust into a Nature which had lost its spirit, we should have to put it somewhat as follows: As long as you remain in your ordinary waking consciousness, your environment will seem to have been robbed of spirit. But if you plunge consciously into the region embraced by the Earth, where you can behold the power of the star-gods in the silvery light of the Moon flowing and surging through the Earth, you will come to learn—no longer with the earlier spontaneity but only by human effort—that external Nature is everywhere permeated by spirit-beings and bears the gifts of the gods within herself as spirit-beings and elemental spirits.

This was the consolation which the priests of the Mysteries could give their people in olden days; they made them see that plants are not just beautiful but are really permeated by the weaving of the spirit; that the clouds do not just sail majestically through the air but that divine-spiritual elemental beings are active in them—and so on. It was towards the spirit of Nature that these Initiates led the men who depended on them for guidance.

Thus at a certain point in man's evolution the task of the Mysteries was to make it clear that when Nature appeared to have lost the spirit, this was only an illusion of ordinary waking consciousness. Actually, spirit was to be found everywhere in Nature. You see, there was a time when man lived within the spirituality of existence, and through the Mysteries experienced this spirituality even in the sphere which at first sight seemed to have been robbed of spirit. Man was still dependent on the spirit in all that affected him, whether instinctively when he had inner spiritual perception, or by the Mystery-teachings which showed him that Nature also was permeated by spirit.

If human evolution had stopped there, our consciousness could never have experienced one of the greatest blessings of humanity, perhaps the very greatest—I mean the experience of free-will, of freedom. The old mood of soul, with its instinctively experienced spirituality, had to be damped down. Man had to be led to three other conditions of consciousness. The feeling of being embraced by the Earth, which had enabled the old Initiates to attain their star-wisdom and their knowledge of Nature's spirit, died away completely, and man's soul-condition came to include only dreamless sleep, dreaming and waking. To balance this, there were the beginnings of that sphere of consciousness in which freedom can dawn. What we call to-day our waking consciousness, which enables us to enjoy our ordinary life and knowledge, was quite unknown to early humanity. Yet through it came the possibility of pure thinking; we may profess doubts about its existence, but in it lies the only possible basis for the impulse of freedom. Had men never attained this pure thinking—which is actually *pure thinking* and does not, as such, guarantee the actual reality—they would never have reached the consciousness of freedom.

We might say that as humanity developed, man's earlier association with the spirit was veiled in darkness; on the other hand, he acquired those three states of consciousness which led him from spiritual heights into the depths of the Earth. But out of these depths he was to find the original forces for the unfolding of freedom. This quality of soul, with its waking, dreaming and sleeping, had been developing for close on a thousand years, and men had gone far into that darkness where the light of the spirit does not shine but where the impulse of freedom is to be found. Try to realise what human evolution has really been like. There was a time when man looked up to the starry heavens and the knowledge he still had of the stars showed him that their forces lived within him and that he belonged essentially to the Cosmos. But now, man—as spirit—was thrust down to Earth and the Heavens became, so to speak, dark, for the light, though shining down physically from sun or stars, became impenetrable for him. It was as if a curtain had come down, so that he could no longer find any basis for his existence. He could no longer perceive what lay behind the curtain.

We shall see to-morrow how this curtain had existed for a thousand years, becoming thicker and thicker, and how this expressed itself in man's whole mood. Then a light appeared which did penetrate the curtain and to a certain extent the curtain fell away; it was the light that shone forth on Golgotha. In this way the Deed of Golgotha finds its place in human evolution. This Deed, accomplished on the Earth, was to reopen for man the vision of the spirituality of the world which he had once seen in the wide spaces of the Cosmos. Christ, by passing through the Mystery of Golgotha, was to bring into man's life on Earth what had in earlier times been seen in the Heavens. The divine-spiritual Being of Christ was to descend and live in a human body, so that He might bring this light in a new way to men who could no longer leave the Earth.

We are only just beginning to understand the Mystery of Golgotha, and the future evolution of the Earth must consist in this Mystery being ever more deeply understood, so that the radiance spreading from the Mystery of Golgotha will change more and more from an inward to a cosmic radiance and will gradually irradiate everything perceptible to man.

But we shall be able to talk of this in greater detail only if we lay some further foundations for it to-day. Now something which was once a living fact in human evolution is, in a sense, returning. The priests of the Mysteries possessed, as I have told you, the power of contemplating the influence of the Moon; the influence of the Moon bore them up to their astrological Initiation. They learnt how it was possible to be initiated into the secrets of the stars by this means. An important point for the candidate for Initiation was that he should feel as though gravity were of less importance to him than it normally was. He felt that he weighed less. But then he was instructed by the older teachers not to give way to this feeling; when he began to feel lighter he must restore his heaviness by a strong exercise of will. The technique of the old Initiation made it possible for the candidate to allow the weight which was lost by the influence of the Moon to be restored by an effort of will; and as a result the wisdom of the stars shone forth. Thus every tendency in man at that time to overcome gravity was used to develop the will to hold fast to the Earth by the power of his own soul. But since this exerting of the will acted as a kindling of an inner light, it

shone forth into the Cosmos and he could attain knowledge of
cosmic spaces. When Spiritual Science throws its light on
these matters, it is possible accurately to describe how this old
consciousness came into being.

Now there is always a tendency for what existed in such
men to recur; there is a sort of atavism, an inheritance, of
things long past. It recurs just because men themselves return;
and when this relation to the Moon appears in men who live
at a time when, because this deep sleep is a thing of the
past, such a relation should not occur, it appears as somnam-
bulism, especially as ordinary sleep-walking. Then they do
not combat this increasing sense of lightness by exerting the
forces of their soul, but they wander about on roofs or at
least get up out of bed. They do with their whole being what
only the astral body should properly do. Something which
has now become an abnormality was in earlier times an asset
which could be used to attain knowledge. It was quite appropriate that popular usage should call such men 'moon-struck',
for this condition of man's being is connected with an atavistic
relation to the Moon-forces which has survived from older
times.

Again, just as man is related, in the way I have described,
to Moon-forces, he is also related to Sun-forces. But they are
active in a more hidden part of man's being and we find
them only indirectly. The Druids of the finest period—not
those when decadence had set in—certainly sought their Sun-
Initiation in this relation to the Sun-forces. Now whereas
astrological Initiation depends on Moon-forces and makes
possible a knowledge of the secrets of the Cosmos, this Sun-
Initiation makes possible a sort of conversation with the
divine-spiritual Beings of the Universe, a kind of Inspiration,
whereas the Moon-Initiation gave only Imagination. Sun-
Initiation is like a listening to the counsel of the spiritual Beings of the Cosmos—certainly a much deeper vision of the
secrets of the world's being than could be given by Moon-
Initiation. This may also recur atavistically, for Sun-activity

exists in every man. But the constitution of man's soul to-day is quite different from that of the past, and his eyes are now specially organised to see only the physical rays of the Sun. As I told you yesterday, in the physical rays of the Sun there is an element of soul and spirit. Modern man does not realise or perceive this. In his attitude to the Sun, present-day man behaves as if he met another man who claimed to possess some inner quality of soul, and said to him: "There is no such thing; if you move your arm, it is a mechanical process like that of a lever; the muscles act as cords and when they are drawn tight the lever comes into action. That is the mechanism of it."

That is really how men behave nowadays in regard to the Sun; they see only the external-physical; that is, the physical light. But when the physical light of the Sun's working penetrates into us, the spirituality of the Sun's being penetrates also. By means of a sort of inner concentration—not acquired in the way described in my book, *Knowledge of the Higher Worlds* but possessed atavistically like some elemental force— a man can nowadays (and by nowadays I mean our present epoch of history which may of course extend for some thousands of years) cease through inner concentration to be strongly receptive to the physical working of the Sun but may, on the contrary, become receptive to its spiritual activity. Then his sight is changed. When this atavistic capacity appears, he sees differently from the ordinary way. When we look into a mirror, we see the reflection of what stands in front of the mirror. Just because the mirror is not transparent, it can reflect in this way. Now when a man's soul is constituted in such a way that, even when in full possession of all his senses, instead of looking into the Sun and seeing the physical sunlight he sees darkness, the darkness then becomes a sort of mirror which reflects his immediate surroundings. He does not say to himself: Here I have a plant which has a root which sends forth its leaves, flower, fruit and seed; rather, he says: When I look into the lower part of a plant, I see in it

an elemental spiritual wisdom which makes it solid and
permanent; if then I look further up the plant, I see how that
quality is gradually overcome and how the plant strives to
create alternatively a contraction and expansion in the formation of leaves, and finally strives upwards in the blossom, as
though transformed by fire. In this way the life of the plant
is reflected in the darkness, which is however spiritual light.

Jacob Boehme possessed this atavistic power when he looked
at the plant and saw the quality of *salt* below, the *mercurial*
in the middle and the *phosphoric* above. Thus we can see in
the spirit of a man such as Boehme, who was a natural Sun-
Initiate, a capacity belonging to an earlier period of civilisation, that primal civilisation before there was any reading or
writing. You completely misunderstand him if you read works
such as the *Mysterium Magnum*, the *De Signatura Rerum* or
the *Aurora* and do not see that in this stammering presenta-
tion there is something quite similar to what I described in
relation to the Druids. Boehme was not initiated in an external sense, but his Sun-Initiation rises within him like a
repetition of an earlier earthly existence. We can trace this
into the very details of his biography.

There are still deeper forces which can be active in men,
the forces of the outermost planet of our solar system.
Modern astronomy does not regard it as the outermost since
it has added two more—though even orthodox astronomers
are worried because the movement of the moons does not
properly fit,* but since it is the spatial arrangement with
which they are concerned, they have added Uranus and
Neptune. These, however, cause trouble because their moons
are a little crazy compared with the ordered moons of Jupiter
and other planets. In reality one must say that, for a living,
concrete grasp of the planetary system, Saturn is the outermost planet. Now just as a man can be under the influence
of the Moon-forces which I described in detail, or of the Sun-

* The moons of Neptune and Uranus move in the opposite direction
to the satellites of other planets.

forces, which I only outlined, he may also be under the influence of Saturn-forces. The activity of Saturn, as it rays into the planetary system and thus also into man, is like a cosmic historical memory. Saturn is, as it were, the memory, the recollection, of our planetary system, and if you want to know anything about the history of that system, you cannot really get it by astronomical speculation.* Even external science is becoming rather desperate about all this because nothing fits. But the problem is not rightly tackled.

We have often spoken among ourselves about the so-called theory of relativity and the idea that it is never possible to talk of absolute motion; that there is nothing but relative motion. We can either say that the Sun moves and the Earth stands still, or that the Earth moves and the Sun stands still—as we have done in modern times. It makes no difference which one says, since everything is relative. And on one occasion here in Stuttgart, at a meeting of the Anthroposophical Society when we were talking about relativity, a supporter of the theory showed his audience clearly how it is all the same whether you take a match and strike it on the box, or take the box and move it past the match : in either case you light the match. This was meant as a serious scientific statement, and there is nothing to be said against it. Perhaps some simple soul might have thought of nailing the box to a wall—and then we should have had a little bit of "absolute". We might somehow have moved the whole house and we should have had relativity again—but this might have been difficult! Yet if one takes the whole physical world, Einstein is quite right in saying that within the world there is nothing absolute, everything is relative. Unfortunately he stops at relativity, and it is just this relativity that ought to lead us on to look for something absolute, not in the physical world but in the spiritual. Everywhere nowadays, science—were it only rightly

* See *The Spiritual Individualities of the Planets.* Lecture given at Dornach, 27th July, 1923.

understood—offers us entry into the spiritual world. It is not a question of amateurish but of genuine exact science, and genuine science—except that it is not thought through to the end even by its experts—will lead to the spirit. Ordinary physical investigation cannot really tell us what this Saturn of our universe is. Saturn is in a sense the memory of our planetary system; everything that has occurred within that system is preserved in Saturn, and a Saturn-Initiate can learn of all those happenings.

Now just as our relation to the Moon can appear in a one-sided form in men as an inheritance of an older period of human evolution, with the result that they become sleep-walkers, or, again, as the spiritual forces of the Sun may emerge so that a man will not see the sunlight with open eyes but will see into the darkness in which Nature is mirrored, and then he will see as Boehme did—in the same way it is possible to experience our relation to the forces of Saturn, which work particularly on the head and implant in the human being a passing memory during his life on the Earth. These Saturn-forces can appear in a peculiar way, and just as we can talk of "Moon-men" who are the ordinary sleep-walkers, and of "Sun-men" such as Boehme, or in a lesser degree, Paracelsus, so we can also speak of a Saturn-man. This is what *Swedenborg* was. His is another case which should worry ordinary science—though it does not!

Swedenborg was master of the ordinary science of his time and was regarded as an authority. Up to his fortieth year he was thoroughly orthodox in his views and said nothing to which ordinary science might take exception. Then he suddenly became befogged. Actually we ought to say that the Saturn-forces became active in him, though people with an ordinary materialistic outlook say that he went mad. But it ought to make us pause to realise that there are so many surviving works of his which are recognised as scientific and are being published by a Swedish Society. The most distinguished scholars in Sweden are occupied just now in publishing his works—works, that is, written, shall we say, before he attained spiritual vision. There is something unpleasant in having to deal with a man who up to his fortieth year was the most brilliant man of his age and after that must, to put it mildly, be called a fool!

Actually Swedenborg did not become a fool, but, at a particular moment, just after he had reached the heights of ordinary science, he began to see into the spiritual world. When this power of vision reached his head—the organ he had developed to so high a level—and when it was influenced by the spirituality of Saturn, he had his own special power of vision, not the vision of Boehme who saw the inner secrets of Nature mirrored in the darkness, but direct vision into the etheric, where the patterns of a higher spirituality appear. And thus he was able to give his own descriptions of them— though he did not actually see what he imagined he had, for the spirit-beings to whom he was referring are different. Nor on the other hand was it a mere earthly reflection of these spirits; he saw *etheric forms and the activities of spirits in the etheric*. He saw in the ether of the Earth the *deeds* of the spirits, though not the spirits themselves. Whereas Boehme saw reflections of Nature, Swedenborg saw what was accomplished in the etheric by the spirits whose activity was all he could see. Thus when he describes Angels, it is not Angels whom he sees but etheric forms. Nevertheless, these forms were actually the work of Angels—a picture of the activity of Angels. We must always keep our eyes on the reality of such things. And whereas it would be an error to claim that Swedenborg saw the spiritual world as such (that was not his peculiar power), yet it was a reality that he saw.

The ordinary sleep-walker does something real, does with his physical body what he ought to do only with his astral body. Boehme saw with his physical body, particularly with his eyes, which were organised in such a way that he could exclude the physical and see into the darkness, but in that darkness he saw the light, the mirroring of Nature-spirits.

Swedenborg did not see mirror-pictures, but etheric pictures of a spiritual existence of a higher order. Here we have an upward process from the sleep-walker who, being permeated by spirit, does not see but acts automatically, through what I may perhaps call the natural second sight of Boehme who saw not the external side of Nature but the mirror of its inner side, up to Swedenborg who saw not mirror-pictures but reality in the etheric, the picture of activities which proceed in higher spiritual regions.

You see then in what way we can speak of man's past and present, and how in the so-called abnormal conditions there is a sort of inherited survival which we must try to understand. When we can see the past in this light and see also what survives from the past into the present, we shall be able to get some idea of mankind's future with the help of a deeper understanding of the Mystery of Golgotha. This is what we shall attempt in the lecture to-morrow.

LECTURE 3

MAN IN THE PAST, THE PRESENT AND THE FUTURE

Stuttgart, 16th September 1923

You will have been able to realise from the lecture yesterday that a certain state of consciousness, which was an actual experience to men of earlier times, has to some extent been lost. I told you that the special sort of waking consciousness we have to-day, which consists predominantly in more or less abstract ideas or at the best in shadowy pictures, did not then exist in the same form, and that in its place there was a kind of waking-dreaming, or dreaming-waking. This was not experienced as we experience dreams but as a living picture which corresponded pretty well with spiritual reality. There was a condition of sleep which, though it was dreamless, left an after-effect of the kind described, and there was a third state of consciousness beyond this which was experienced as a resting in the surging Moon-forces, forces which, reaching under the Earth, lift man out of earthly gravity and allow him to experience his cosmic existence. The essential, point about these older conditions of soul was that they allowed man to experience his cosmic existence. In our ordinary everyday consciousness there is only a shadowy image left of that older state of consciousness—a shadowy image that is noticed by very few and is mostly entirely unheeded.

I will try to describe this survival of a primeval state of consciousness. When we observe our dreams—chaotic as they are—we find that all sorts of experiences drawn from earthly existence flow into them. Things long forgotten crop up altered in many ways, even things which passed unnoticed at the time. The times, too, at which events took place may be thoroughly confused. But if you look more closely into the details of a dream, you will discover the remarkable fact that in essence practically everything which crops up in it is related to the happenings of the last three days. You may perhaps have a dream about something that happened to you twenty-five years before; you may dream of it in all its vividness, though somewhat altered in detail. But if you study it closely you will always discover something of the following sort : in this dream about an event of twenty-five years before, a character appears whom we will call Edward, and you will find that you have somewhere heard the name casually in passing, or your eye has caught it as you were reading. In the details of a dream, even the remotest, there is always some relation, however insignificant, to something which has happened during the last three days. The reason is that we bear within ourselves the events of the last two, three or four days—the period is of course approximate—in a quite different way from those which occurred earlier.

Our perceptions are, as you know, taken up into our astral organism and our ego-organism, and the events thus perceived do at first live in direct connection with our consciousness. What we have experienced in the course of three days— that is, when at least three days have passed—goes more intensively into our feelings. Ordinarily we do not notice these things, but they are realities all the same. The reason is that all we perceive or think, which is taken up into the astral organism and the ego-organism, has also to be somehow imprinted upon the etheric body, the body of formative forces, and at least to some extent even upon the physical body. This process takes two to four days, so that we have to sleep two or three times on anything we experience before it is imprinted on the etheric and physical bodies. Only then is it firmly fixed in the etheric body so that it may be a permanent memory. Thus in man there is a perpetual inner reciprocity, a sort of struggle, between the astral and etheric bodies, and the result is always that what we have experienced consciously is imprinted into the denser, more material elements of our being. After three or four days, what was at first only a transitory sense-experience is transferred into the body of formative forces and into the physical body.

But how little of what I have been describing actually comes into men's consciousness nowadays! Yet it is something which is perpetually taking place in the life of the human body and soul. Every experience of which we have been aware has to wait three or four days before it is fully our own. It fluctuates between the astral and etheric bodies, and cannot decide—one might say—whether it has really been impressed into the etheric and into the physical body.

This is something of extraordinary significance. Remember that basically our true being is only our ego and astral body. We cannot really claim that the etheric body is our own property. In this materialistic age people talk as though the etheric and physical bodies were theirs, whereas actually they belong to the whole Cosmos. And so when in the course of three or four days, what our ego and astral body have experienced is passed on to the etheric and physical bodies, it is then part, not only of ourselves but of the Cosmos. It is only for three days that we can claim any action of ours in the world as significant for ourselves alone. After that we have, as it were, imprinted it on the Universe, and it rests within the whole Universe and belongs not only to us but also to the gods.

In very early periods of human evolution, as a result of that state of consciousness which is now lost and which was deeper than sleep, men had a definite impression of this remarkable fact, and the Initiates were able to give information about what lay behind it. Particularly in the epoch of which I spoke yesterday, the Egypto-Chaldean epoch, it was only a vague feeling that men had. But the priests were initiated into the real nature of the fact. Whereas nowadays Initiation must be a purely inner experience of soul and spirit, at the most with symbols and rites of a physical nature only, in those earlier days Initiation was an external process and the effects of that external process passed over into man's inner being. To take one example: when a man was to be initiated, for three or four days he was put by the Hierophant who was initiating him, into this state of consciousness which we have now lost. The purpose of this was to enable him to see for himself what happens during these three days in the world external to him, and how it finds entrance into the real being of man. The Initiate was enabled to see what happens to an idea, to an experience or a feeling, before it becomes a man's own property.

Our materialistic attitude to the world to-day affords us no conception at all of the extraordinary significance of the wisdom that lay within this condition that is so deeply concealed from us. I can perhaps best explain to you what was accomplished in the three days of this Initiation during that dim condition of consciousness if I remind you first of our ordinary dream-life. Certainly we must study it very carefully. If, as we obviously should, we discard every superstition, if we try to get inside this dream-life with an attitude based purely on what we might call scientific method, there is still something extraordinarily profound involved.

How is this dream-life really revealed? There are of course many kinds of dreams, but let us keep for the moment to what consists largely in the recollection of past experiences. Pictures of these experiences arise in dreams. How do they arise? You are aware that they appear radically transformed. This transformation may go a very long way; for instance, we may take the case of a tailor who in his ordinary life has never had the occasion of making a Minister's state robes; he may have made a number of coats and been very proud of them, but for all that he has not the slightest chance of making such a robe as he now dreams he makes. In a dream like this there may be a number of different influences at work. For instance, the man may in a former life have been the attendant of a Roman magistrate and among his duties had to help him on with his toga. A dim feeling of all this survives and what a man experiences in this life may be coloured by what streams over from a previous one.

This is just an example of how the content of dreams may be altered; the important fact is that they undergo the intense transformations we all know. One must really ask what is contained in these dreams, what is at work in them. It is external events which give the occasion for this type of dream, but the external events make their appearance in a wholly altered form.

The reason for this is quite beyond the conception of our ordinary scientific ideas. The sort of law which we should recognise as scientific, the laws we look for in the external world by our method of observation and experiment, cease to be valid as soon as we pass inside the skin of a human being. We should be very much mistaken were we to assume that the natural laws laid down in the laboratory were valid within the human being. Not only are the substances transformed within our organism when we consume them in the ordinary course of nourishment, but the laws of the substances are also changed, down to the smallest atoms. What appears in our dreams is not just the abstract reflection of some reality; in our dreams we see the weaving of the organic laws within which man has his being. Dreams are much closer to us than is our normal abstract thinking; they show the way in which external substances act within man. Our dreams are a protest against the part of reality that is shackled within the laws of Nature. From the time you go to sleep until the time you wake, you live in a world where according to the scientist everything is controlled by these laws. Actually the moment you enter, even to the slightest degree, into the spiritual world through your dreams, your dream-experience arises as a protest against the laws of Nature. Dreams cannot run their course in the way of external events, or they would be very much like actual waking life. Dreams which emerge from real sleep are in their make-up a protest against the laws of Nature, and they concern us much more intimately.

In this regard modern investigators of a materialistic turn of mind have made some interesting discoveries. Some of you will know a book by a man called Staudenmaier, entitled *Experimental Magic*, which appeared a good many years ago and is typical of the spiritual constitution of many modern scientific thinkers. Staudenmaier wanted to find out if there is any reality in the spiritual world. Of Anthroposophy he admitted that he knew only what its opponents had written. People don't like studying Anthroposophy; they find it difficult, particularly if they are typical scientific thinkers of to-day.

Staudenmaier attempted, by spiritualistic methods, to get into the spiritual world. He dulled his consciousness until he was in a sort of mediumistic state; then he began automatic writing and was surprised that he wrote a lot of nonsense which did not at all agree with what he knew about reality. In particular, the fact that spirits seemed to be speaking to him did not agree with it! He knew that was impossible and yet what he wrote assured him that spirits were speaking. He was appalled by the lies that these non-existent spirits told him. You should read in his book all the incredible lies which flowed into his writing. He became—to use no worse a word— just like a medium, and he did not know what to make of it all. A friend advised him to give the whole thing up and to lead a normal, sensible life and go out shooting. So he did, and he went out after magpies; but even there he found that whatever it was he had stirred up inside himself continued its activity, and he could not rid himself of it. If he looked up at a tree, he saw, not a magpie but a fearful dragon with terrible fangs, which looked at him with horrifying eyes. The same things happened everywhere, and he lived in an inner struggle to get himself back into a normal condition.

I mention all this because here we have experimental evidence that there is an immediate protest against the external order of Nature as soon as we are not merely dreaming while awake but are using this device to contact and arouse the inner being of man. Obviously we regard it all as lies. When we have thought of a man as a friend and as a decent fellow, and if after he has got into this mediumistic condition we see him putting out his tongue at us or making long noses, then inevitably we say that the spiritual world is lying and that this experience is simply that of a dream. Now there is something in this. Whenever man approaches the spiritual world inside himself, within which everything inside his skin is enclosed, there is an immediate protest from this sphere against the natural order. It is not surprising that when a man enters it with undeveloped faculties of judgment, all kinds of elemental beings appear and create delusion. But there is always this protest against the natural order when we approach the spiritual; and ordinary dreams make this clear.

We ought to realise that we then enter a quite different order of being, and, even though it appears only in the fleeting form of the dream, it is all the same a protest against those admirable laws of Nature which we establish by laboratory experiments. This is the first step into the spiritual world where we immediately find the protest against natural laws, which are, as it were, robbed of their dignity as soon as we penetrate a little into man's inner being.

The old Initiates knew very well through their three days' Initiation that there is not only a natural order, but that within and behind that natural order there is a spiritual one. It is moreover still possible for anyone who has acquired some knowledge of Initiation to penetrate with modern methods into these things and to pass through the experiences of these three days, when for the first time he experiences a really fearful torment of the soul. When dreams begin to weave their forms we actually enter a world where the laws of Nature collapse and just because the ordinary laws no longer hold good, their interrelations change, however many recollections of ordinary life may still be effective. If we have come to regard natural laws as the last word, we find ourselves face to face with nothingness. It is painful, almost tragic, for a modern man, as he passes through Initiation, to experience entry into a sphere of being where this protest against the laws of Nature is encountered; he feels that everything he had got from his intellect, and which was determined by the laws of Nature, is swamped. His soul can no longer breathe because he has been too much accustomed to the natural order. He finally realises that an altogether different world is pressing in from a quite different direction. This is no longer a natural but a spiritual order, which is throughout permeated with what in the depths of our present-day human conscience we experience as a *moral world-order*. He gradually learns that on the one hand there is the order of Nature perceived by the senses, for which the laws have been established by natural science; on the other hand, if he moves out of this natural order, he moves into a world that protests against the natural order. As he experiences this protest, a sort of luminous water of life pours round him and he can once again breathe—this is the moral order which ultimately expands into the spiritual.

The highest knowledge gained by the ancient Initiates was when they discovered the protest against the physical world-order and saw the true moral world-order extend into the physical. It is indeed experienced in a much weaker degree during the three days described : whatever we experience in the external world, whether actions or feelings, takes three or four days to be imprinted on our organism. But when the process is completed, the imprinted form is not like that which we experienced externally; it becomes an impulse demanding a moral expression very different from the natural order. If we could see how our experiences have changed in our inner being during those three or four days, we should see that what we experienced in its natural form during our earthly existence has been imprinted in our eternal being and is no less real than it was in the external world. But now it lives within us as the impulse of a moral world-order by means of which we may move further over the ocean of life. Thus we carry the results of what we have experienced naturally as the moral foundation for our later life.

In recent periods of human evolution, however, when man plunged into that "lower sleep", if I may call it so, that Earth-embraced sphere, he plunged into the outer ether. There his experiences find their compensation. He is not merely set within the moral world-order as regards the direction of his inner life; in that lower sleep he is set within the moral order of the Cosmos. Since this deep sleep has been lost to our forms of consciousness and we now have only a very faint echo of it in the three-days' experience described, this contact with the Cosmos has been lost also. Indeed, we should have been gradually thrust out of the self-subsisting moral world-order if a particular event had not occurred in the course of Earth-evolution. The experience undergone by the older Initiates so as to be able to tell men what happens during those three days, was undergone as a unique world-event, as an event in world-history, by the Christ Being who descended from spiritual worlds into the body of Jesus of Nazareth and, though a God, lived a truly human life. That experience of the three days now became available for all mankind. What could previously be discovered in the sleep of deep consciousness, taking place in man not consciously but at least subconsciously, in a natural way, had to be gone through in order that man might find his connection with what was brought about for earthly humanity by Christ in the Mystery of Golgotha. This was the vicarious deed of a God. Man was to take a step upwards in his evolution and to experience in moral form through Christianity what had previously come to him naturally. The Mystery of Golgotha is therefore closely related to the whole meaning of earthly evolution, because of its relation to the evolution of man's consciousness. We can understand what was to be accomplished by the Mystery of Golgotha only if we can look back on what had once occurred naturally and was now to occur *morally*.

In this respect, however, our modern consciousness, which

runs its course between waking, sleeping and dreaming, has not yet attained inner harmony. Since the fifteenth century, when this modern consciousness first received its imprint, it has looked on Nature one-sidedly and has claimed to understand the order of Nature, considering that what is found there constitutes reality. Beyond this reality men will not look; they will not press forward to that strengthened form of human knowledge to which the spiritual reveals itself just as the natural order does. Thus it has become customary to speak of the moral order as of unknown origin. To do this was not strictly honest, since the common view of Nature cannot admit any reality in the moral order. One could, even if a little dishonestly, get over this difficulty by saying that on the one side we have knowledge, on the other, faith; that knowledge cannot become faith nor faith, knowledge; and that the moral order belongs to the realm of faith. Such is the convenient formula which has become customary. The distinction has even come to be regarded as something specifically Christian, though even five or six hundred years ago no genuine Christianity, and certainly not original Christianity, would have admitted the distinction. Even to-day it is not yet Catholic dogma, however much it may be Catholic custom, to distinguish in this way between faith and knowledge.

We cannot get a proper notion of the relation between the natural and the moral-spiritual order because we are not aware of the transition between them; because the dream is not understood which leads out of the natural order and protests against it, thus preparing the way. If we have gone through this preparatory stage, we can make contact with the moral order of the world.

Only an honest view of the past of mankind, and of something which modern man does not yet possess, can lead to a satisfying picture of all this. Failing that, even historical documents of ancient times remain just things which can be studied but convey no real meaning. Now we spoke this morning a good deal about the opponents of Anthroposophy.

I could say much that would be for their good, though certainly not in their favour. The comments of our opponents . . . I often have to recall an anecdote supposed to be based on truth which the famous Professor Kuno Fischer was fond of telling. He used to relate how he had had two schoolfellows —they may have been brothers   with an uncle who was a thorough simpleton. The boys got to the stage of learning logarithms and having to buy log. tables. The uncle caught sight of these tables and when he saw the mass of figures he asked his nephews what they were. The boys were completely at a loss to explain, but at last the young rascals conceived the idea of telling him they were the house-numbers of all Europe. The uncle believed them and finally thought it an excellent idea to be able to know at a glance all the house-numbers of London, Paris, and so on. Now people who are unable to see with insight into the meaning of the ancient documents are like the old uncle with his log. tables. Our modern historians who edit these ancient documents do not tell us much more about them than the uncle did about logarithms when he took them to be the house-numbers of Europe. We must make it clear to ourselves how far their interpretation, based on present-day abstract thought, is removed from the real spiritual facts. We must have the determination to do that, or we shall never be able to see how man has developed into the present out of a past when he was very different.

We are living at a time when all sorts of inner conflicts must arise from our present-day experience of sleeping, waking and dreaming, if we are in the least capable of real self-observation. Just as men lost the real knowledge of that deep sleep which was so significant for them that the Initiates had to explain its nature to them, so in modern times our ordinary sleep tends to crumble to pieces. I do not mean that in the future men will dream the whole night through, but rather that their dreams will be dulled. Just as man has passed since olden times from that "waking dreaming" to our modern abstract thinking, our present-day chaotic dreams will be dulled, and that duller kind of sleep will become normal. Dreams will no longer extend into our consciousness, which will be overlaid entirely by our present-day form of abstract logical thinking. But then a super-consciousness will emerge, already apparent to anyone who can understand these things. This super-consciousness is concerned with the human WILL and with the effects of the will when it acts on the nervous system. If with the help of Initiation-knowledge you observe the unrestrained way in which human will is developing, you will be able to see how various psychological manifestations, sometimes going as far as actual physical illness, are really the herald of a form of consciousness higher than our present waking consciousness.

But there is something beyond this which men will not yet be able to experience unless they can actually acquire spiritual science : a science, that is, which needs a quite different sort of thinking from the normal and is in reality far more practical than the theoretical attitude to life, which is in fact completely unpractical. This spiritual science adds an inner living power of thinking to ordinary abstract thinking. Yet this is not something we can arbitrarily add or neglect; it occurs because an organism is coming into being within man which did not exist in earlier times and of which only the first foundations have so far emerged. The way in which the blood circulates through man's limbs, his arms, legs, hands and feet, is continually changing. What we often call "nervousness" (a nervous state) nowadays is an expression of the fact that a higher condition is striving to make its way into man, but that he is unwilling to accept it because of its strangeness, and this produces a restlessness which will cease only when he makes the new consciousness his own.

Thus we can visualise three further states of consciousness towards which man is making his way : a dulled dream life, waking, and a heightened state of waking. All the turmoil and upheaval which show themselves even in external conditions to-day are due to the fact that men are trying, for the most part quite unconsciously, to fight against something that is approaching humanity from the spiritual worlds. It is struggling to make its way especially into the human *will*. We shall have to understand—as nowadays we do not—that as soon as the spiritual comes into action, we pass at once into a sphere where a protest is uttered against natural laws. We shall also not properly understand the Mystery of Golgotha unless we can rise to the realisation that the full import of that Mystery cannot be attained by our ordinary knowledge. To grasp its full meaning we have to develop a new faculty; we have to pass with right understanding beyond mere dreaming, which indicates a natural process, and penetrate to an understanding of the other side of being. It is from the side of the spirit that we have to acquire the elements of understanding adequate for future comprehension of the Mystery of Golgotha. What we must do is to set our experience of the present in this way between the past and the future, and so feel ourselves as a sort of bridge between them. Thus we shall increasingly achieve the understanding required for the use of spiritual truths alongside the natural.

It is easy to understand our ordinary illusions, just because the things that are false are so uncommonly logical. We do not suspect that falsehood can be so logical. What could be more logical than to argue as follows : first observe how long it takes some particular geological stratum to reach a particular thickness, then, if we are dealing with another stratum, divide the smaller into the greater thickness and multiply it by the time taken by that stratum to form, and so reach the conclusion that some epoch, the Silurian or Devonian for instance, was twenty or 200 million years ago. The arithmetical calculation is quite correct and there is nothing to be said against it. It is only ordinary logic that is here deceiving us.

This sort of logic always reminds me of the logic one of the greatest mathematicians of all times applied to his own life.

When he had already reached a considerable age he suddenly became ill with some kind of lung trouble; and seeing that he had had a good deal to do with doctors, he had the idea of calculating how many tiny abscesses would have to be got rid of in order to shake off the lung trouble. His calculations about the further development of the illness showed him that it would take fifteen years, and then he would be cured. But ... he died two years later. That was the reality; the other was only logic.

The same sort of thing applies to the relationship between reality in the Cosmos and our ordinary logic. Things are very easily proved by logic, and the logic is perfectly sound. It is just as sound as if we calculated as follows: Our heart goes through certain phases of development; in a definite period it will have reached a definite condition; then we calculate how long it would take to reach that condition and the answer is 300 years. Then we can calculate backwards 300 years and see what our heart looked like 300 years ago. Unfortunately we were not alive, at least as physical beings, 300 years ago, and we shall not be alive 300 years hence. Equally the Earth did not exist in those past ages that are worked out by the geologists. The destinies undergone by the Earth can be known only in spiritual terms. That is the distressing thing about modern science: it can prove so logically what is really an illusion, and its proofs tell us nothing about reality.

Human beings to-day, though people do not realise it consciously because they refuse to be aware of it, are living with the unconscious fear that they are on the way to losing touch with truth. We can see this fear manifesting itself in various forms. Fundamentally, the people who base their philosophy of life on materialism are very ill at ease. They are always harassed by anxiety about the limits they have set themselves, for their cherished limits create appalling obstacles to living a fully human life. People already feel intuitively that if they have nothing more than the natural order to rely on, they cannot draw real life from it; above all, that the ideas derived from this natural order cannot lead them to any genuine artistic and religious experience or ideas.

We must always remember that our existing religious systems originated in the times when men were dependent on that deep sleep I have described for their understanding of the Cosmos. All our religious institutions derive from those times: the religious institutions, yes, but not the Mystery of Golgotha. That is independent of any religious view; it stands within the Earth's evolution as a fact; and it has to be grasped by those conditions of consciousness that are still in course of preparation. For centuries now, even millennia, the religiously creative side of man has lain barren and the same is true of real artistic capacity. With rare exceptions we have to live on what we can get from various cultural revivals. We do not possess any original power of creation. But that is what is seeking to make its way into this age, and the general unrest typical of our civilisation to-day is something like the birthpangs of a new age, a new age in the scientific and artistic spheres but also in the social, religious, and moral spheres. The future of mankind—that is what we must strive to take to heart. There has never been a time when humanity has been less disposed to listen to Initiation-knowledge and yet never a time when humanity has been in greater need of it.

That is why I wished particularly to speak to you about the past, present and future of humanity from the point of view of the evolution of consciousness. Of course, in three lectures I could do it only in outline, but you can work out within your own hearts what I have told you. Because our consciousness lies closest to our own being, it is there that men can become most easily fruitful and be stirred towards spiritual experience. In order that present-day man may develop into a man of the future, what we need is not any materialistic experience but spiritual experience. Ever since we have been victims of abstract thinking and ideas, our inner habit is really such that anyone participating in our present culture must have the same sort of impression from any talk of the spirit as the simple old uncle in the story about the log. tables, and will interpret all the powerful evidence for the entry of the spiritual as if it were like the house-numbers of Europe. The analogy is a little far-fetched but if you remember what I have told you, you will understand what it means. Our normal attitude to life, or rather our ordinary judgements about life, penetrate into all our scientific thinking and produce there a philistinism and banality raised to the nth degree, even a moral hypocrisy claiming scientific validity. If there is any, even the slightest, sign of the entry of the spiritual, it is assumed to be something which intelligent human reason, according to this materialistic view, can only call "mad".

There is a good story, founded on fact, which also illustrates this attitude. At the beginning of the forties of the nineteenth century the old philosopher Schelling was called from Munich to Berlin. He had held his peace for several years, but a high reputation had preceded him. People looked forward to lectures on philosophy of a more positive kind, as opposed to those he himself called negative. Anyway, in these lectures at Berlin University he was to deal with the spiritual development of man, the essence of religion and the Mysteries, in a much deeper fashion than anyone had done hitherto.

When Schelling began his lectures, the front rows were occupied by the most brilliant intelligences, the professors of the various subjects, the heads of the teaching departments and the most distinguished representatives of spiritual life —certainly not mere callow students, who had to sit at the back. They were all waiting—as far as they were able to wait—to see what Schelling's great reputation would accomplish. As the lecture proceeded, the faces of the audience grew longer and longer. Schelling did in fact speak in a remarkable way about the spirit; just at the moment when materialism was reaching its climax and coming to its fullest flower, he spoke of the spirit. As he spoke, the faces grew appreciably longer because the audience had no idea what he was after.

Trendelenburg, well-known later on as a philosopher, who was sitting in one of the front rows, said he thought he had understood a little, though most of it was beyond him; but he was not even sure he had understood that little!

Then, some days later, two of the people who had been present at the lecture happened to meet. There had been a good deal of discussion among Schelling's hearers, and these two had taken part in it, wondering why on earth he had been called to Berlin, since not a word of what he had said was intelligible. But one of them now had the answer: Schelling's daughter had got engaged to the son of the Minister of Education! So everyone could understand why Schelling had been willing to come to Berlin. The whole thing was explained!

It may seem strange to tell you these things, but I am obliged to talk to you in this way. For the form of thinking characteristic of the present day is so far removed from the sort of thinking proper to Anthroposophy, which is moreover not just a whim of ours but an absolute necessity for man's future unless he is to fall into decadence. Only this new form of spirituality will be able to experience fully the three stages of consciousness which will emerge in the future: namely, a damped-down dream-sleep, ordinary waking, and a heightened consciousness. Otherwise man will never be able to experience his humanity properly in future lives on Earth. For the gods wish out of present threefold man to form the threefold man of the future, as they have formed the present threefold man, the dreaming, sleeping and waking man, out of the former threefold man who dreamt in pictures, slept, and on waking experienced the after-effects of his sleep, and also slept deeply. In this present age of freedom, as I have so often explained to anthroposophists, we must resolve by our own free knowledge to live towards the goal laid down for us by the divine Powers of the world. If we do that we shall not only think, we shall above all feel, in the right way about the past, present and future. Then we shall also have the right will with regard to this life on Earth, in accordance with the divine-spiritual ordering of the world—from the past, through the present, into the future.

This is what I wished to talk about, and with these words I will bring our studies to a close, not however without expressing a wish that to-morrow a discussion may begin here which will show that in the Anthroposophical Society some desire exists to promote a fully living consciousness in this Society of what man in his fullness is to be—the *whole* man who must be comprehended as including man of the past, man of the present, and man of the future. For these three are also one. What man has been in the past, what he is in the present, and what he is to be in the future, will embrace in face of the divine World-Order the whole being—*anthropos*. But in order to strive for this there must be an enthusiastic, heart-felt grasping of Anthroposophy to lead us to the true *anthropos*, the whole man, man in his fullness.

THE SUN-INITIATION OF THE DRUID PRIEST
AND HIS MOON-SCIENCE

Dornach, 19th September 1923

From the most varied points of view—the point of view in *Occult Science* is only one of these—I have indicated how in a certain very early condition of our planet, Sun, Moon, Earth (indeed the other planets too, only this will not concern us to-day) were one whole, and how we must speak first of a departure of the Sun from the one whole, Sun-Moon-Earth; and then at a much later epoch, of a departure of the Moon.

All these matters have, of course, their external aspect, derived from sense-conceptions. But they have also an inner aspect, which is this: that Beings are bound up with such an existence, with Sun-existence, with Moon-existence—Beings who also on their part liberated themselves from the one whole with the separation of the Sun and entered into an entirely different kind of existence in the Cosmos. So that as regards the further evolution of the Earth we cannot merely speak of a detached Sun, exerting its physical and etheric influences on the Earth, but, when it is a question of taking the spiritual element of the Cosmos into account, we must speak of a Sun population, of Sun Beings, who although they were once united with the Earth now lead an existence outside the Earth-evolution—an existence that extends far beyond this Earth-existence, and is much more sublime.

It is exactly the same in the case of what may be called the Moon population. And when we were describing the spiritual side of such cosmic processes, it was necessary to point to the fact that within the Earth-evolution itself there once existed a primordial wisdom. But this primordial wisdom did not, of

course, consist of concepts which, as it were, floated around
in the air; it proceeded from Beings who do not assume a
physical body in the human sense, but who, as the result of
the instinctive clairvoyant forces possessed by man at that
time, did nevertheless live in man; it proceeded from the
Beings who continued their existence on the Moon, after the
Moon as an external cosmic body had separated from the
Earth. We must therefore say that within the Moon-being, not
in the light that the Moon radiates back as reflected sunlight,
and not in all the rest of what the Moon radiates back from
the Cosmos, but in the inner being of this Moon-existence
there live Beings who were once the founders of the primordial wisdom among Earth men. These are the Beings who
passed over into the figures of myths and sagas in picture
form, who did not assume forms perceptible to the ordinary
consciousness; they are primordial Beings to whom we look
back with wonder and awe, even if we only discover them
externally as the real foundations of the myths, sagas—primordial Beings to whom the intellectual forces of present
humanity can attain only by great exertion through the
development once again of Imagination, Inspiration, and so
on. But there did remain, at all events within humanity itself,
something that was a kind of unconscious memory. And then
in the different evolutionary epochs of human civilisation, by
which I mean, of course, the more ancient epochs of civilisation, these unconscious memories appeared in man's life of
feeling and in his whole constitution of soul, so that when we
survey civilisation we can speak of a Sun civilisation and a
Moon civilisation. These are, as it were, consciousness-
memories of something that in earlier times worked in a far-
reaching sense as Nature-forces in man; and what man perceived of them is only an appendage, reminiscent of growth
forces, forces of inner organisation.

On the basis of such conceptions we are able to penetrate
in some degree into the Druid culture. With the means access-
ible to-day to external science man will ask in vain as to what

was the real soul-constitution of these Druid priests. (I might just as well call them Druid sages, for both are expressions entirely suited to that age, although of course they did not exist then.) What was it that lived in the impulses by means of which these Druid priests guided their people?

What is often narrated in history, and indeed often sounds terrible, always signifies something that was active in the epochs of decadence and degeneration. What I am going to describe here invariably refers to what preceded this epoch of degeneration, and was active when the civilisation was in its prime. For these cromlechs, these Sun circles, in what they truly represent, draw attention to what existed in the epoch when the Druid Mysteries were in their prime. And with the means given us by anthroposophical Spiritual Science, we can in a certain way even to-day penetrate into the whole manner and mode of working of these Druid priests. It may be said that they were everything to their people, or rather their tribe. They were the authorities for the religious requirements, so far as one can speak of religious requirements at that time. They were the authorities for the social impulses, and also, for instance, for the healing methods of that time. They united in one all that later on was distributed over many branches of human civilisation.

We obtain a right perspective of this Druid culture—and it is quite correct to use this expression—only when we realise that its essence is to be found in an epoch preceding that which echoes to us from those mythological conceptions of the North that are connected with the name of Wotan or Odin. What is associated with the name of Wotan really lies later in time than this epoch when the Druid culture was in its prime. In the orbit of wisdom that points to the divine name of Wotan or Odin we must recognise something that comes over from the East, proceeding in the first place from Mysteries in the proximity of the Black Sea. The spiritual content of these Mysteries flowed from the East towards the West, in that certain "colonising" Mysteries, emanating from the Black Sea and proceeding westwards, were founded in the most varying ways.

All this, however, streamed into a culture that must be called sublime in a deeper sense, into a primordial wisdom, Druid wisdom. This Druid wisdom was really an unconscious echo, a kind of unconscious memory of the Sun and Moon elements existing in the Earth before the Sun and Moon were separated from it. Initiation in the Druid Mysteries was essentially a Sun-Initiation, bound up with what was then able to become Moon wisdom through the Sun-Initiation. What was the purpose of these cromlechs, these Druid circles? They were there essentially for the purpose of a spiritual observation of the relation of the Earth to the Sun. When we look at the single dolmens we find that they are really instruments whereby the outer physical effects of the Sun were shut off in order that the Initiate who was gifted with seership could observe the effects of the Sun in the dark space. The inner qualities of the Sun element, how these permeate the Earth, and how they are again radiated back from the Earth into cosmic space—this was what the Druid priest was able to observe in the single cromlechs. The physical nature of the light of the Sun was warded off, a dark space was created by means of the stones, which were fitted into the soil with a roof stone above them and in this dark space it was possible by the power of seeing through the stones to observe the spiritual nature and being of the Sun's light.

Thus the Druid priest standing before his altar was concerned with the inner qualities of the Sun element so far as he needed the wisdom that then streamed into him—streamed in, however, in such a way that the wisdom had still the character of a Nature-force—for the purpose of directing and guiding his people.

But we must always bear in mind that we are here speaking of an epoch when men could not look at the calendar to see when it was right to sow, when this or that grain of seed ought to be entrusted to the soil. In those ages men did not look at a book in order to get information about the time of the year. The only book in existence was the Cosmos itself. And the letters that formed themselves into words arose from the observations as to how the Sun worked on one or other contrivance that had been erected. To-day, when you want to know something, you read. The Druid priest looked at the action of the Sun in his cromlech, and there he read the mysteries of the Cosmos. He read there when corn, rye, and so forth were to be sown. These are only instances. The impulses for all that was done were read from the Cosmos. The greater impulses, which were needed, one may say, to complete the yearly calendar, were obtained from observation within the shadow of the Druid circle. So that in this age, when there was nothing that was derived from the human intellect, the Cosmos alone was there. And instead of the printing-press man had the cromlech in order to unravel from out of the Cosmos the mysteries it contained.

Reading the cosmic book in this way, men were therefore concerned with the element of the Sun. And in contradistinction to the Sun element, they perceived the Moon element. The forces which were then concentrated in the Moon were once united with the Earth. These forces, however, did not wholly withdraw; they left something behind in the Earth. If there had been Sun-forces alone, rampant, growing cells only would have arisen, life elements, always with the character of small or large cells. The diversity, the formation, does not emanate from the Sun-forces, but from the Moon-forces working together with the Sun-forces.

When he exposed himself to all that his circles, his cromlechs could reveal to him, the Druid priest did not receive the mere abstract impression which we to-day receive, quite rightly, when in our way—that is to say in an intellectual way—we enter into the things of the spirit. For the forces of the Sun spoke to him directly. In the shadow of the Sun the spiritual Sun-nature worked into him directly, and it worked far more intensely than a sense-impression does on us to-day, for it was related to far deeper forces. As the priest stood before his place of ritual, observing this Sun-nature, his breathing changed even as he observed. It became unliving, it was blunted, it went in waves so that the one breath merged into the other. He, with all that he was as a human being through his breath, lived in what was given as a resulting influence of the Sun. And the outcome was no abstract knowledge, but something that worked in him like the circulation of the blood, pulsating inwardly through him, kindling his human being even into the physical. Yet this working into the physical was spiritual at the same time, and the inner stimulations he experienced—these were really his knowledge.

We must conceive this knowledge in a far more living way, as far more intense—we must conceive it as living experience. Moreover, the Druid priest received it at certain times only. With a lesser intensity of life it could be kindled in him every day at noon; but if the great secrets were to be revealed, the priest had to expose himself to these influences at the time which we now call the season of St. John. Then there arose what I may call the great wave of his knowledge as against the lesser daily waves. And while, through the Sun-influences which he thus caught up on Earth in a peculiar and artificial way, he experienced what he felt as his Initiation—his Sun-Initiation—he became able also to understand the forces which had remained behind as Moon-forces in the Earth when the Moon had left it. Such was the Nature-lore he gained under the influence of Sun-Initiation. What was revealed on the surface of things was unimportant for him, but what welled forth from below as the Moon-forces in the Earth, this was important. Through the principle of Initiation, whose relics, as we have seen, are preserved in these strange monuments to-day, he placed himself in a condition to gain knowledge. And the knowledge he gained was of all that works in Nature, especially when in the sky at night-time the stars stood over the Earth, and the Moon travelled across the heavens.

The Sun-Initiation gave the Druid priest the spiritual impulse, and as a result he had his science of Nature. Our science of Nature is an earthly science. His was a Moonscience. The underlying Moon-forces, as they ray forth in the plants from the depths of Earth, as they work in wind and weather and so forth—these he felt. He felt them, not in the abstract way, as we to-day—having an earthly science—feel the forces of Nature. He felt them in all their livingness.

And what was thus livingly revealed to him, this he felt as the elemental beings living in the plants, in the stones, in all things. These elemental beings, having their dwelling-place in trees and plants and so forth, were enclosed in certain bounds. But they were not those narrow bounds that are set to man to-day. They were far wider. His science of Nature being a Moon-science, the Druid priest perceived how the elemental beings can grow and expand into gigantic size.

From this resulted his knowledge of the Jötuns, the giant-beings. When he looked into the root-nature of a plant beneath the soil, where the Moon-forces were living, there he found the elemental being in its true bounds. But the beings were ever striving to go forth and grow outward, gigantically. When the kind of elemental beings who lived beneficially in the root-nature, expanded into giants, they became the giants of the frost, whose outward physical symbol is in the frost, who live in all that sweeps over the Earth as the destructive hoar frost and other destructive forces of the frost-nature. These were the loosened root-forces of the plants which lived within the frost, as it swept with its giant forces over the Earth, working destructively; whereas in the root-nature the same forces worked bounteously and beneficially. And what worked in the growth of the leaves, this too could grow to giant size. Then it lived as a giant elemental being in the misty storms that swept over the Earth, with all that they contained in certain seasons—with the pollen of the plants, and so forth.

And what lives gently, modestly, as it were, in the flower-forces of the plants, when this grows to giant size, it becomes the all-destroying fire.

Thus in the weather-processes the Druid priests beheld the forces of being expanded into giants—the same forces that lived within their right limits in the kingdoms of Nature. The chosen places where we find these old heathen centres of ritual show that what they received on the one hand through the Sun-circles and the cromlechs, was developed into the Earth-knowledge which was thus made possible. They developed it so as to be able properly to observe the mysterious working and weaving of wind and weather as they sweep over the Earth—the working together of the water and the airy nature, the hoar-frost oozing forth from the earth, the melting dew. It was through the Sun-Initiation and the knowledge of the Moon-beings that there arose this most ancient conception which we find at the very foundations of European culture.

Thus the Druid priest read and deciphered the cosmic secrets which his institutions of the Sun-Initiation enabled him to gain from the Cosmos. Thus, stimulated by the Sun-Initiation, he gained his knowledge from his science of Moon-nature. But with all this the whole social and religious life stood in close connection. Whatever the priest could say to the people arose on the spiritual foundations of this element in which the people lived. We see it best of all in what the Druid priests possessed as a science of healing. They saw on the one hand the elemental beings contained within their bounds in the various growths and products of the mineral and especially of the plant kingdom. Then they observed what happened to the plants when these were exposed to frost, exposed to the influences which the giants of the storm and wind carry through the airy spaces, or again, exposed to the seething of the fire-giants. They studied what the giants of frost and hoar-frosts, the giants of the storm, the fire-giants, if loosed and set free, would do to the plants. At length they came to the point of taking the plants themselves, and imitating within certain limits all that was indicated in outer Nature as the influence of the giants. They subjected the plants to a certain process, to the freezing cold process, the process of burning, the process of binding and solution.

The Druid priests said to themselves: "Looking out into this world of Nature we behold the destructive working of the giants, of frost and storm and fire. But we can take from these giants, from the Jötuns, what they spread so awkwardly and clumsily over the world; we can wrest it from them; we can harness once more within narrow limits these loosened forces of the Moon."

This they did. They studied what takes place in the thawing earth, in storm and wind, in the fierce, seething heat of the Sun. All this they applied to the Sun-nature which lived in the plants and which they themselves received in their Initiation. And in so doing they created their remedies, their healing herbs and the like, all of which were based upon the fact that the giants were reconciled with the Gods. In those times each single remedy bore witness to the reconciliation of the foes of the Gods with the Gods themselves.

What man received immediately under the influences of Sun and Moon, just as it was offered by Nature herself, this would be a food-stuff. A medicine, on the other hand, would be something that man himself created, in that he continued Nature beyond herself, harnessing the giant-force to place it in the service of the Sun.

We must imagine the Druid civilisation spread out over a great portion of Northern and Central Europe about 3,000 or 3,500 years ago. Men had nothing at all similar to writing. They had only this cosmic writing. Then into all this there spread from the East, to begin with from a Mystery in the region of the Black Sea, what is now contained as an insoluble riddle for the ordinary consciousness in the Norse Mythology, associated with the name of Wotan.

For what is Wotan? The Mystery from which this Wotan culture proceeded was a Mercury Mystery, a Mystery that

added to the impulses of Sun and Moon the impulse of Mercury. One might say that that old civilisation was there in a
Sun- and Moon-radiant innocence and simplicity, untouched
by what could be told to mankind through the Jupiter impulses. Only away in the East these Jupiter impulses were
already present. From thence they now spread, colonising,
towards the West. Wotan-Mercury carried his influence west-
ward.

Here at the same time we have thrown light upon the fact
that Wotan is described as the bringer of the Runes, the Runic
art of writing. He was the bringer of what man drew forth
from himself in the first primitive way of intellectuality as an
art of deciphering the universe. This is the very first entry of
intellectualism, the Wotan impulse. Thus one might say that
the Mercury-, the Wotan-nature, was now added to the Sun-
and Moon-natures.

Wherever this Wotan impulse worked itself out fully, everything that was present from earlier experiences was influenced
by it. It all received a certain impulse from this Wotan
element. For there was one thing, a special secret of the Druid
culture. We know that at all places things arise that do not
belong there. Weeds grow on the tilled land. We might say
that the Druid culture recognised as the good plants of civilisation only the Sun and Moon qualities, and if, hastening
forward as it were to a later time, the intellectual element
already then arose, they treated it as a weed. Among the
many remedies the Druids had, there was one against the
Mercury quality of deep thought and introspection. Strange
as it may seem to us to-day, they had a remedy against this
habit of sinking into one's inner being, or as we should say, of
pondering on one's own salvation. The Druids wanted man to
live with Nature and not to sink into himself, and they regarded as sick and ill anyone who even attempted to express
anything in signs or the like, unless it were merely to imitate
the things of Nature in a primitive form of art. Anyone who
made signs was diseased and must be healed. Indeed he was

then considered as a black human being, he was not white. Yes, my dear friends, if we with all our present knowledge were transposed into the Druid culture, we should all be sent to hospital and cured.

And now from the East the Wotan civilisation brought this very illness. The Wotan civilisation indeed was felt as an illness. But it also brought, with a power grown truly great and gigantic, what had formerly appeared as an abnormality, an unhealthy introspection. Into the midst of what had formerly been taken only from the cosmic writing, it brought the Rune. So that man now transferred his intellectual element into the signs he made. It brought in all that was felt as a Mercury culture. Thus it was no wonder that what proceeded from the Wotan culture, distilled from the best forces that were in it, viz., the Baldur-Being, the Sun-Being, was felt and thought of as one united not with life, but with death. Baldur had to go to Hel, into the dark forces of Death, the dwelling-place of Death.

Moreover, to begin with, men pondered most, as we can see from the traditions of the Edda, not on the question of how this Baldur, son of the Wotan forces, should be freed from Hel—for this is really a later conception—but on the question of how he should be healed. And at length they said : We have many means of healing, but Baldur, the intelligence proceeding from the Runes of Wotan—for this there are no remedies, and it can only lead to death.

Thus we see once more what I have pointed out to you from so many points of view in the study of human evolution. In olden times the instinctive knowledge of mankind knew nothing of the significance of death, for men remembered the pre-earthly life and knew that death is only a transformation. They did not feel death as any deeper incision than this. Above all there was no such thing as the tragedy of death. This only entered in when the Mystery of Golgotha approached, which became indeed a redemption from the fear of death. In the Baldur legend you see the most visible description of how, with the entry of intellectualism, there comes that mood of soul which reckons with death, and you see what thus entered into human evolution.

Thus what had been seen in the death of Baldur, who could not rise again, was only healed once more in the way of soul and spirit, when the Christ-figure who could rise from death was placed over against him.

It is wonderful how in the North, through the influence of the Mercury-forces on the Sun- and Moon-forces, the perception of the Christ-impulse was prepared. In Baldur, the God who falls into death and cannot rise again, we see the forerunner, in the North, of Christ, who also falls a victim to death, but who can rise, because He comes directly from the Sun. Baldur, on the other hand, the Sun-force coming from Wotan, is the Sun-force reflected back by Mercury, radiating forth from the signs which man makes out of his intellect.

Thus we see how evidently all these things evolve in the Northern regions, where man still appears to us living and reading in the Cosmos, seeking for his religious, social and medical conceptions from the Cosmos, until at a later stage he passes over to dwell with the Earth-forces. From his sacrificial stone the Druid priest gazes at the configuration of the shadow of the Sun, and reads what appears in the shadow, representing the spiritual aspect of the Sun. Then we approach the time when the Sun-Being, the Sun-nature that had been caught up, as it were, in the cromlechs is drawn in abstract lines, called rays. We approach the time when the relationship of what lives in root and leaf and blossom with what lives in frost and wind and fire is recognised at most in a chemical sense. Giants and elemental beings alike are transformed into "forces of Nature". And yet in our forces of Nature no more is contained than the giants of ancient time. We are only unaware of the fact and feel immensely superior. It is a straight line of development from the giants to the forces of Nature. These are the latter-day children of them. Man who lives today in a highly derived, i.e., an unoriginal, civilisation, cannot but be deeply moved when he looks at these scant relics of the Druid age. It is as though he were to behold the hoary ancestors of what is living in this present time.

To go more into detail, we too to-day speak of medicine and remedies in a strangely abstract way, very intellectually, describing abstractly their mode of preparation. All this we must imagine transformed into something altogether living if we would look back on the way the Druid priest regarded his remedies. For he felt the Sun-forces which he knew so well and which in plants and other products of Nature he treated with the forces of the giants. All this was altogether living for him. From the giants he wrested the forces of preparation to transform the plants into medicaments. He knew that in so doing he did something for the whole Cosmos. Then he gazed on man himself. Through his peculiar knowledge of man he most intimate parts of the natural man, e.g., in the dream-recognised the symptoms coming forth, as it were, from the imaginations that arose, the vague, unconscious flickering-upward of the deeper human nature into consciousness under the influence of these remedies in which the giant-forces were subdued and held in check. He recognised how these things worked in the human being into whom they were instilled. Thus he had on the one hand his Loki in the wild influences of the outer fire, and on the other hand what he had taken away from Loki in order to transform this or that plant by a combustion process into a medicament. From the way this worked within the human being, he then beheld the Loki-force in man. For here it was disarmed. And the Druid said : That which out there in the world of the giants is working with threatening danger and destruction works healingly when brought in the right manner into the inner man. Poisonous forces as it were on a large scale become healing forces when brought to the right place.

Thus the Druid in his way perceived the varied forces and workings of Nature. Thus he was within the spiritual whereby he sent forth the religious, social, medical and other impulses into his community. Thus in that time the ancient primeval wisdom which the Moon Beings, so long as they were here, had cultivated on the Earth, and which was now no longer here directly, since they themselves had gone with the Moon —this primeval wisdom was preserved through Beings that were found and known by a kind of Sun-Initiation in the way I have described to you to-day.

Writings

1. Works written between 1883 and 1925
2. Essays and articles written between 1882 and 1925
3. Letters, drafts, manuscripts, fragments, verses, inscriptions, meditative sayings, etc.

Lectures

1. Public Lectures
2. Lectures to Members of the Anthropsophical Society on general anthroposophical subjects.
   Lectures to Members on the history of the Anthroposophical Movement and Anthroposophical Society
3. Lectures and Courses on special branches of work:

Art: Eurythmy, Speech and Drama, Music, Visual Arts, History of Art

Education

Medicine and Therapy

Science

Sociology and the Threefold Social Order

Lectures given to Workmen at the Goetheanum

The total number of lectures amount to some six thousand, shorthand reports of which are available in the case of the great majority.

Reproductions and Sketches

Paintings in water colour, drawings, coloured diagrams, Eurythmy forms, etc.

When the Edition is complete the total number of volumes, each of a considerable size, will amount to several hundreds. A full and detailed Bibliographical Survey, with subjects, dates and places where the lectures were given is available.

All the volumes can be obtained from the Rudolf Steiner Press in London as well as directly from the Rudolf Steiner Verlag, Dornach, Switzerland.